JOHN CLARE'S BIRDS

JOHN CLARE'S BIRDS

Edited by
ERIC ROBINSON & RICHARD FITTER

Illustrated by
ROBERT GILLMOR

Oxford New York
OXFORD UNIVERSITY PRESS

Oxford University Press, Walton Street, Oxford OX2 6DP

London Glasgow New York Toronto
Delhi Bombay Calcutta Madras Karachi
Kuala Lumpur Singapore Hong Kong Tokyo
Nairobi Dar es Salaam Cape Town
Melbourne Auckland
and associate companies in
Beirut Berlin Ibadan Mexico City

British Library Cataloguing in Publication Data
Clare, John
John Clare's birds.
I. Title   II. Robinson, Eric   III. Fitter, Richard
828'.709   PR4453.C6
ISBN 0-19-212977-5

Set by Western Printing Services Ltd
Printed in Great Britain by
Butler & Tanner Ltd, Frome and London

CONTENTS

INTRODUCTION

Clare as Poet

John Clare's reputation as 'the finest poet of Britain's minor naturalists and the finest naturalist of all Britain's major poets'[1] came about through a slow maturing both of his poetry and of his powers of observation. Not until his middle period, the years 1824 until 1832, did he demonstrate consistently his characteristic voice both as poet and naturalist, and it is in those years that most of his best poems about birds were written. In an attempt to show the public how Clare really wrote before he was tidied up by his earlier editors, Eric Robinson and Geoffrey Summerfield published some of his writings about birds, both in verse and prose, in *Selected Poems and Prose of John Clare* (Oxford, 1967). That volume included 'The Wren', 'The Fern Owls Nest', 'The Sand Martin', 'To the Snipe', 'The March Nightingale', 'The Nightingales Nest', 'The Sky Lark', 'The Ravens Nest', 'The Moorehens Nest', 'Pewits Nest', 'Crows in Spring', 'Emmonsails Heath in winter', and 'The Robins Nest' as well as prose passages about the land rail or corncrake, the robin, the nightingale, and birds' nests. Now, in this collection devoted entirely to Clare's writing about birds, the editors have sought to add to the number of Clare's poems and prose-writings of his best period before the poems of the asylum period where, though many excellent qualities exist, they are often of a different character. Though the collected edition of Clare's poems for the Oxford English Texts is well under way, it will still be some time before all of it is published and, since Clare is a voluminous poet, it will be very bulky. In the meantime there seems to be a justification for putting forward still another selection of Clare's work that will not duplicate anything in the volume mentioned above or in Robinson's and Summerfield's edition of *John Clare: The Shepherd's Calendar* (Oxford 1964) where also many excellent lines about birds are scattered.

Clare's earliest poems about birds tend to stem from proverbs:

[1] James Fisher, 'The Birds of John Clare' in *The First Fifty Years: A History of the Kettering and District Naturalists' Society and Field Club* (Kettering, n.d./1956).

And magpies that chatter no omen so bad
The dreams of my being a bride
Odd crows that are constantly fixt in my pad*
Plain provd what bad luck woud betide

[A5, 17]

or from conventional misinformation, as in 'The Wagtail's Death'
(B1, 20), where he confuses the cuckoo with the hawk. Two early
sonnets 'To the Robin' and 'To the Nightingale' show little more
direct observation than any eighteenth-century run-of-the-mill ver-
sifier. Clare was not yet writing with his eye on the object. Even in his
early poems, however, from time to time we see him using his own
eyes rather than his memory of other poets' lines, as when he writes:

And chirping sparrows dropping from the eaves
For offald curnels that the poultry leaves
Oft chittering signal calls of danger nigh
At skulking cats and dogs encroa[ch]ing bye

Here the dialect word 'chittering', as is so often the case with Clare,
brings precision, just as the participial adjectives 'skulking' and
'encroaching', the latter with its memories of landowners en-
croaching on the commons, accurately suggest the creeping move-
ments of the sparrows' predators while at the same time creating
sympathy for the sparrow itself. In such lines Clare begins to free
himself from those conventional poetical associations of birds
where, for example, the nightingale is symbolic of ruined love and
the cuckoo of marital treachery, but he has not yet reached the point
where he is justified in asking:

Why is the cuckoos melody preferred
And the nightingales sick song so madly praised[1]

It is perhaps strange to reflect that while Clare continued in his
early poems to write with a certain second-hand staleness about
birds, he was, in terms of time, closest to the days of his boyhood
passion for bird's-nesting recalled so vividly in the poems of his
maturity, as, for example, when he speaks of climbing the oak for the
puddock's nest and finding the dust that rubbed off from the bark

---

* path.

[1] E. Robinson and G. Summerfield, *Selected Poems and Prose of John Clare*
(Oxford, 1967) p. 68.

against his chest tasting bitter in his mouth,[1] or the bird flying up under the broken rails

> Frit by the boy while scrambling down the bank
> To reach the misty dewberry[2]

While he is young he writes within conventions: when he is mature, his youth returns like a vision of first love. The act of returning to his youth is not simple nostalgia as Clare's poetry develops. The confusions that John Barrell finds in Clare's early poems 'Helpstone' and 'Helpstone Green'[3] cease to be confusions when what is taking place is not simply recollection but re-creation, and it is interesting that Barrell chooses to illustrate Clare's 'new form . . . expressive of his own idea of landscape' from 'Emmonsails Heath in winter', a poem about birds.[4] This is how Barrell describes the 'new form':

Each place exists as a manifold of things seen, heard, smelled, and for Clare each thing exists only as foreground; he does not detach himself from the landscape as Cowper does, or post himself on a 'commanding height', but describes only what is immediately around him. The attempt, then, is not so much to describe the landscape, or even to *describe* each place, as to suggest what it is like to be in each place.[5]

In his poems about birds and bird's-nesting written in the later 1820s and early 1830s Clare is at his most acute in evoking 'what it is like to be in each place', but that involves him in the double operation of re-creating what he experienced in the past by focusing more directly upon what he experiences in the present. Birds increasingly become, as Clare matures as a poet, a quality of his environment, and Clare's environment in general was modified as the poet became more and more concerned to stress the particularity and the limits of the world in which he lived. From Helpston and Northborough, apart from his visits to London, Clare seldom ventured more than a few miles, so that his poetic landscape is within walking distance of his two homes. More significant than the geographical confines is the way in which Clare saw those few square miles. He is concerned to stress what is *here*. What is *here* is his own: what is *there* is the world's.

---

[1] A46, 149; A47, 4.
[2] Quoted in John Barrell, *The Idea of Landscape and the Sense of Place, 1790–1840* (Cambridge, 1972) pp. 110–13.
[3] Ibid., pp. 110–13.
[4] Ibid., p. 154.
[5] Ibid., p. 166.

Since he was a boy, he had roamed the then largely unenclosed fens and heaths around Helpston, had worked in the open fields of the village, at nearby lime-pits, in hedging gangs, or in the gardens of a neighbouring great house. His Sundays were spent in walks among the fields, either as a marauding bird's-nesting boy or as a young spark flirting with the local girls. Roaming the countryside at night might be dangerous, since much of it was still under water at this date, but Clare knew his way around, drunk or sober, as well as an old horse knows the high road to home. He knew every brook, every hedge, every tree, every bird's nest – and the landmarks became part of his spiritual gazetteer as we see in such poems as 'Salters Tree', 'Emmonsales Heath', and, most characteristically, 'Remembrances'[1] with its landmark references to 'Langley bush', 'old eastwells boiling spring', 'old cross berry way', 'Swordy well', 'old sneap green', 'puddocks nook', 'hilly snow', 'old round oaks narrow lane' and 'lea close oak'. Such names are scattered over the map of his boyhood.

Names, however, only give in themselves the skeleton of his countryside. The flesh is provided by the sights, sounds and smells associated with those names. Salters Tree and Langley Bush are sketched in the margins of his notebooks, as are gates and streams, and birds and shells. All these things are limited to what he actually saw in his neighbourhood. When, in his madness, he assumes the language of Burns and writes of mountains and shielings, his poetry loses focus and becomes again derivative. But in the bird poems of his mature years he makes us follow him, on hands and knees, through the undergrowth of Royce Wood or Puddocks Nook, till we almost touch the bird's nest with our noses:

> Hark there she is as usual lets be hush
> For in this black thorn clump if rightly guest*
> Her curious house is hidden – part aside
> These hazel branches in a gentle way
> And stoop right cautious neath the rustling boughs
> For we will have another search today
> And hunt this fern strown thorn clump round and round
> And where this seeded wood grass idly bows
> Well† wade right through . . .[2]

* guessed.   † We'll.

[1] Robinson and Summerfield, *Selected Poems*, pp. 163, 166, 174.
[2] Robinson and Summerfield, *Selected Poems*, p. 74.

The absence of punctuation leaves the language to control its own movement, to present us with pauses, moments of concentration, obstacles until the final release to which the movement has been building up in 'Well wade right through . . .'. The precise location of the nest – 'this black thorn clump', 'These hazel branches', 'this fern strown thorn clump' (and how that repeated 'clump' makes us catch our breath), 'this seeded wood grass' are directions appropriate for a gipsy or a nesting schoolboy. We get the sense that we are being shown not a nest but one particular nest, and what happens in 'The Nightingales Nest' is apparent in other poems on similar subjects:

> Just by the wooden brig a bird flew up[1]

or:

> Well in my many walks I rarely found
> A place less likely for a bird to form
> Its nest – close by the waggon road and on the ground
> With scarce a clump of grass to keep it warm
> And not a bush to guard it from harms way
> And yet so snugly made that none may spy
> It out save accident and you and I[2]

So the focus is brought down to a few blades of grass at the side of the waggon road, while the conversational tone of the opening words not only reinforces the sense of intimacy taken up five lines later by 'snugly' but gives us the pleasant surprise of having the nest pointed out to us before our eyes. The structure and materials of the nest, the number of eggs and their coloured markings, even the 'rough and powdered rind' where the woodpecker 'knocks and craunches' are pointed out to us in Clare's bird poems. Once or twice James Fisher catches him in a countryman's exaggeration, as when he speaks of a dabchick remaining 'under water for 10 minutes together' or a clutch of 'more than thirty' mallard's eggs, but usually he seems to be right on top of what he is describing and he brings his reader alongside him to look at nature with his eyes.

On the other hand, once Clare moved outside the narrow circle of what he knew, he was lost in the immensities of infinity:

---

[1] 'The Yellow hammers nest', A54, 224.
[2] 'The Pettichaps Nest', A46, 155.

To hunt birds nests on summer morns
So far my leisure seemed to run
Ive paused to wonder where I'd got
And thought Id got beyond the sun

*   *   *

And when again I left the town
To the worlds end I thought Id go
And oer the brink just peep adown
To see the mighty depths below   [A47, 'Birds Nesting']

So it is that sometimes in Clare's poems, the intimate is strengthened by the remote, the remote by the intimate. The corncrake however brings both together, by introducing its mysterious disembodied call into the familiar landscape of Helpston:

Ive read in books but found it not
Ive talked with men of mickle skill
To hunt it Ive in thickets got
But all remains a mystery still   [A47, 'Birds Nesting']

In still other poems, the birds reflect Clare's sense of loneliness, his timidity or even his persecution by the barbaric unfeeling elements of his society. Clare's bird poems therefore do not side-track the reader into some diversionary interest but rather deal with some of the poet's central preoccupations.

Nevertheless, James Fisher has pointed out the remarkable extent of Clare's knowledge of the birds of the Soke of Peterborough. Though Fisher was acquainted with only one, admittedly the most important, of the four lists of birds compiled by Clare, he was still able to state that 'the poet knew from personal observation about 145 wild birds, of which 119 can be identified with reasonable certainty as county records – 65 of them "first records"'.[1] The ornithologist must consult this excellent essay for himself.

What Fisher does not underline, however, is the variety of Clare's observations. For example, Clare was something of a pioneer in his interest in bird song. Whereas, in his early poems, doves coo and swallows twitter, owls whoop and magpies chatter in a conventional way, Clare soon demonstrates his familiarity with the countryman's

---

[1] Fisher, op. cit., p. 27.

equivalents for other bird calls – not just the 'sweet jug jug jug' of the nightingale, but also the firetail's 'tweet tut', the spider catcher's 'eejip eejip', the chiff-chaff's 'chipichap', the cuckoo's 'cuck cuck', the robin's 'tweet', the quail's 'wet-my-foot', and the fern-owl's 'whew' – but also more exact representations such as his lines on the wood-pigeon:

> And sits for hours at 'coo coo coo'
> Still ending stuntly with a 'huff'
>
> [A47, 19]

It is in 'The Progress of Rhyme', however, that Clare makes his most ambitious effort to capture bird song, on this occasion the song of the nightingale:

> The more I listened and the more
> Each note seemed sweeter then before
> And aye so different was the strain
> Shed scarce repeat the notes again
> Chee chew chew chew and higher still
> Cheer cheer cheer cheer more loud and shrill
> Cheer up cheer up cheer up and dropt
> Low tweet tweet tweet jug jug jug and stopt
> One moment just to drink the sound
> Her music made and then a round
> Of stranger witching notes was heard
> As if it was a stranger bird
> Wew wew wew wew chur chur chur chur chur
> Woo it woo it could this be her
> Tee rew tee rew tee rew tee rew
> Chewsit chewsit and ever new
> Will will will will grig grig grig grig
> The boy stopt sudden on the brig
> To hear the tweet tweet tweet so shill*
> Then jug jug jug jug [till a]ll was still
> A minute when a wilder strain
> Made boys and woods to pause again
>
> [A53, unnumbered]

Such a passion for exactitude must have seemed strange to Clare's contemporaries, though perfectly comprehensible to the modern ornithologist. Clare also comments on the imitation of the nightin-

---

* shrill.

gale's song by the thrush and the blackcap (see below, pp. 42, 58), distinguishes the call used by the nightingale summoning its young to feed (p. 44), describes the harsh noise made by the jay as a warning call (p. 13) and discusses at length those birds which can be taught to imitate the human voice (p. 12). He is probably one of the first naturalists to take such precise notice of bird calls, their form, the occasions when emitted and their different purposes. But he never loses his poetic feeling as can be seen in his marvellous couplet on the call of the heron:

> Cranking a jarring mellancholy cry
> Thro the wild journey of the cheerless sky[1]

or when he talks of the night-hawk's cry as 'the whistle call of robbers'. His is a remarkable power. While he claims to be different from the naturalist in his need 'to look on nature with a poetic feeling', he never allows his poetic sense to produce slipshod observation.

If we consider the characteristics of bird flight, Clare is equally acute. Fisher praises the accuracy of his remarks about the flight of skylarks, swallows, green woodpeckers, lapwings, kestrels, and several other birds. Even when, in Fisher's opinion, Clare confuses the swift with the swallow, he is able to determine that it is the swift to which Clare is referring by his accurate description of flight. Much of the vigour of Clare's poetry is carried, or projected, in the verbs of movement associated with bird flight. 'Emmonsails Heath in winter'[2] and 'The crow goes flopping on from wood to wood' are both excellent examples in which Clare uses vigorous verbs of motion such as 'flaps', 'swing', 'bouncing', 'flit', 'flopping', 'wherries', 'whew', 'dashes', 'suthers', 'mounts', 'sails', 'whirls', 'fluttering', and 'swees'. When he writes of the green woodpecker he is always particularly evocative. Even a short prose note on the kestrel in a list of birds is full of feeling:

KESTREL

said to be the species that hangs in the air on trembling wings and is a beautiful object in the blue sky of a summers day

Whether he deals with song, flight, eggs, nest-construction, feeding habits, albinism, the capacity of birds for being tamed, or several

---

[1] *The Shepherd's Calendar*, ed. cit., p. 33.
[2] *Selected Poems of John Clare*, p. 138.

other aspects of bird behaviour, Clare is always worth listening to. It may be the thrush using a pebble to break snail shells (A61, 7), the lapwing leading the shepherd away from his nest (A61, 8), 'The partridge dusting in the milking shed' (A61, 22), the hen gathering her chicks under her wing while the kite hovers overhead (B4, 63), the pigeons, disturbed by the farmer's boy, that 'thunder from the turnip field' (A61, 128), the magpie pulling hair for her nest from the heifer's back (A57, 52), the swallow washing herself in the smoke from the chimney-stack (A41, 88),[1] or the hen moving her nest further up the bank to escape the storm (A45, 46). Always his senses are alert. Clare's extensive knowledge of birds was not won from books. David Powell's Catalogue of the John Clare Collection in the Northampton Public Library (1964) records among the volumes in Clare's library a Natural History of Birds (Bungay, 1815), which he used as a check-list for his own observations, John M'Diarmid's Sketches from Nature (1830), Robert Mudie's The Natural History of Birds (1834), and a copy of Gilbert White's Natural History of Selborne (1825 edition), presented to him by his publisher, J. A. Hessey. Only the last of these could have helped Clare to make more detailed observations of bird behaviour. The Bungay book was out of date when it was published, while Robert Mudie's book was published after Clare's best bird poems had been written.

Clare had no respect for book learning when it came to things of nature and was not overawed by authorities: 'Mr Pennant says he saw the buisness of Geese pulling baere and that they pulled gosslings that were not above 6 weeks old   I have no hesitation in saying that Mr Pennant is a Liar' (see below, p. 91). In his own nature-notes he always makes clear what he has seen for himself and what he takes on report, as in his comment upon the method employed by the young cuckoos to remove other eggs from the nest (pp. 13-14).

As the study of Clare is more seriously and thoroughly undertaken than in the past the originality of the man becomes more and more startling. In a forthcoming book, George Deacon will show the importance of Clare as an early collector of ballads, dance-tunes, and broadsides and as interpreter of the folk tradition; Margaret Grainger has prepared a scholarly edition of all Clare's natural history prose writings. Clare has much to say to the social historian

---

[1] Cf. the Guardian, 'A Country Diary', 8 September 1976.

and yet has been almost entirely overlooked in that area, though his comments on the events of his time are often not what we have been led to expect from an agricultural labourer. In particular his observations upon religion are very challenging. We have attempted in this book to build upon the base laid by James Fisher and J. W. and Anne Tibble to extend among general readers an appreciation of Clare's sensitive response to birds.

Clare as Naturalist

Clare was in many ways a man both behind his times and in advance of them. The 1820s and 1830s were a time, like our own, of devastating change, both agricultural and industrial, but Clare was unlucky in that his contemporaries were carried along with the tide of change whereas our period is generating a fierce resistance to the economic onslaught on the environment. Had Clare remained a sane and free man for a few years longer he might have been part of the protest launched by Carlyle and carried to the end of the century by Ruskin. As it was, he appeared to his contemporaries to be backward-looking, harking back to the previous century, although we, 150 years later, are able to recognize that he could see through the fashionable dogmas to what was actually happening in the country-side. Clare was not entirely unselfconscious of his role as a writer about the English landscape and its flora and fauna. He had read Gilbert White, loved and revered Thomson and Cowper, and ransacked English literature from Chaucer to Chatterton for telling descriptions of natural life. He knew that he saw more clearly than most people who lived around him that the flats and levels of his native heath

> To common eyes they only seem
> A desert waste and drear;

and that worse still, to a stranger like one of his publishers, John Taylor, one of Clare's favourite spots, Lolham Brigs, might appear to be only a 'dull line of ponds, or rather one continued marsh, over which a succession of arches carries the narrow highway'. Today even the most receptive visitor must confess that the Helpston countryside is undramatic, though its openness creates vistas and the eye is continually drawn to the horizon and thence upwards to the clouds. The little towns and villages that dot the plain are also full of charm, built from the famous Northamptonshire stone that has been quarried for centuries and has produced some of the finest masons in English history. The churches too are exceptionally beautiful and every few miles will throw up another spire beside a group of trees, sometimes corpulent like a farmer, sometimes so slender that one almost ceases to breathe for fear the slight addition to the wind, which blows unchecked in these parts, should cause it to topple. Clare saw it all, from the painter's vista to the outlook of a hare hidden among the grasses. Clare's vision is varied and embraces many ways of seeing. He is much more complex than at first sight he seems to be. When Raymond Williams in *The Country and the City* distinguishes between the writing of Gilbert White, on the one hand, and Clare and Wordsworth on the other, the distinction confuses rather than illuminates. It is not true, for example, as many passages in this book will show, that White's remark that 'The ousel is larger than a blackbird, and feeds on haws ...' represents a different viewpoint from Clare's or a separate style of writing. Much of Clare sounds exactly like this, though it is true that at other times Clare's observations may be modified by strong feeling. Many of Clare's poems about birds have a poetic intensity which stems as much from his studious involvement with the details of their nesting habits and the characteristics of their eggs as it does with any 'projection of personal feeling' into his observation. It is also quite clear that Clare sometimes wrote prose notes about birds and then worked them up into verse with a minimum of change in mood or atmosphere. And as for linking him with Wordsworth, as both Williams and Bloom do, Clare's poetry is totally distinct from Wordsworth's both in method and message. Clare was conscious of a tradition of nature-writing before him. He was better read than most critics acknowledge. He is both unique and a part of an evolving sensibility.

It is instructive to compare Clare's writings with those of Richard Jefferies, the next great rural observer, when the storm of the enclosures had subsided. Although the countryside of the 1870s and 1880s was still much nearer to the eighteenth century than it is to the second half of the twentieth century, there was none of the bitterness that was provoked by the massive destruction of the medieval agricultural ecosystem that Clare witnessed at first hand. Jefferies, in a sense, accepted what Clare protested at, because he never saw England as it was at the beginning of the century.

Besides being a poet of growing stature, Clare was also a brilliant observer of the natural scene. Indeed the combination of poet and field-naturalist has never been bettered in our literary and scientific history. Wordsworth may have been a better poet, though even that is open to question, but he was what we would nowadays call a nature-lover rather than a naturalist. White, largely because he was educated, was a better naturalist, but a far inferior poet. And it is with names of their stature that Clare must be compared. These are his peers. It is interesting to speculate on what would have happened if Clare's patrons had found time to give him the grammar-school education he would probably have had if the medieval church had still been trawling for priests. That he would have written in a more formal grammatical manner is neither here nor there. Would acquaintance with the classics have damped his poetic vision or clouded his vivid perception of the natural world? Maybe we should never have heard of John Clare if he had become a teacher, or even Rector of Helpston. Or would he have made his mark more quickly or more surely? As far as we in the late twentieth century are concerned, we should be thankful for what has come down to us and that no Victorian busybody destroyed his manuscripts. Let us recognize him for what he is, a major figure both in poetry and in natural-history writing – a prophet who can guide us into the next century.

It is as difficult to know what makes a naturalist as what makes a poet. Both are callings, or qualities, that a man either has or has not, and it is hard for non-poets and non-naturalists to understand what makes them tick. Most great naturalists have had their interest from an early age, although some, like Darwin, did not develop it fully until later; others, like Huxley, sprang more or less fully developed from a pupa-like change in their maturity. Clare, however, like White and Jefferies, seems to have been continuously interested in animals and plants from an early age. A great many boys and girls have a childhood interest in wildlife: it is what makes the few carry on into adult life that is so mysterious.

One might perhaps define a naturalist as a man or woman who, as he goes about, in either town or country, is constantly aware, not just of the animals and plants he sees, but also of what they are doing and of their relationship with one another. In a city street the naturalist will pay more attention to the crow that chances to fly over than to the contents of the shop windows; in the country, he will look not just at a wood, but at an oakwood, an ashwood, or a conifer plantation, and will instinctively recognize the plants that grow in them. It has been estimated that there are some 60,000 species of animals and plants in Britain. No naturalist can possibly be aware of them all, especially the smaller species, but he will be aware that they exist, that a grass field is not just a sward of green but a patchwork of grasses and other plants, and invertebrates of all kinds. He will not fail to be aware of the larger and more conspicuous species: ox-eye daisies that stud the roadside bank, stoats that cross the road in front of him, butterflies that flit past, birds that call or fly within his conscious attention. But few naturalists are able to observe these things with a poet's eye, like Clare. Clare differs from White in this respect. Where White devotes his attention to sorting out the three kinds of leaf-warbler, and draws attention for the first time to the existence of the wood-warbler as well as the chiff-chaff and the willow-warbler, Clare is much more concerned with what creatures are actually doing and how they fit into his vision of the countryside. Like most other naturalists, he lists the birds he has seen, but more as one would inventory one's treasured possessions than simply as a scientist.

Nevertheless he is such a good observer that scientific conclusions can be drawn from his observations. Time and again some couplet of his shows keen observation of some quirk of behaviour that the purely scientific naturalists may not have got around to till much later in the century. Druce, the historian of Northamptonshire's flora, was able to identify 135 plant species from Clare's poems and found that no fewer than forty had not been recorded by earlier botanists. Clare's greatest handicap as a naturalist was lack of contact with other naturalists. No naturalist can hope to be completely self-taught, even with access to good books. Inevitably Clare makes mistakes, due to inadequate observation. For instance, as James Fisher pointed out, he confused to some extent the habits, appearance, and voices of the barn and tawny owls, and it is by no means always possible to be sure which owl he refers to in his writings. But this in no way detracts from his achievement. It only means that if he had had the companionship, not just of the sports-loving Artis and Henderson from the big house, but of a fellow naturalist, or better still of a local field club, he would have been that much better a naturalist sooner in his career. His natural ability as an observer and his retentive memory carried him as far as they could, but what a pity he had no Charles Waterton to help him. His patron,

Lord Milton, later 5th Earl Fitzwilliam, was an observer of birds, as his personal diaries from 1829 to 1845 reveal, but apparently the two men were too distant from each other by class and education to discuss their common interest at any length, if at all. Such conversation could not have made him a better poet, but it could have made him a better naturalist and more useful to posterity.

It is impossible to write about Clare as a naturalist without seeing him in his country setting. Few British naturalists, not even White at Selborne, are more closely identified with their own parish. Almost everything Clare ever experienced stems from his childhood at Helpston. We hear little or nothing about what he may have seen or heard in Epping Forest, at Northampton, or even at Northborough. It is the observations of his childhood years at Helpston that are so sharply imprinted in his mind and pour out in his poems and his prose. Here we really are sundered from him, for if you go to Helpston today you will not find the countryside of his childhood. That countryside was largely destroyed by enclosure within Clare's own lifetime. Castor Hanglands and Ailsworth Heath survive as an oakwood and a limestone heath in a national nature reserve but all else has been under the plough for a century and a half. Some of Clare's major poetry is a lament for his lost countryside, the open fields that had been farmed that way since the Middle Ages, the fens, the pastures and Emmonsales Heath. At least we can reconstruct them in our own imagination through the keen and vivid perceptions and memories recorded in his writings.

NOTE ON THE ARRANGEMENT OF
THE SPECIES

How to arrange this selection of hitherto unpublished material on birds by John Clare presented some problems. The order in which birds appear in modern field guides and county avifaunas seems hardly relevant, since it reflects the views of modern ornithologists on how bird families are related to one another in the evolutionary tree. In the eighteenth and early nineteenth centuries evolution had not yet acquired the scientific basis that Darwin and Wallace gave it in 1859. So it did not occur to writers of bird books to use it as a basis for classification. Instead, they tried to arrange their birds on the basis of common characteristics such as hooked beaks or webbed feet, and for the most part followed or adapted the system published by the great Swedish naturalist, Linnaeus, in 1758. Clare, of course, knew nothing of these considerations, and probably would have thought them of little consequence if he had. He was a field naturalist, not a closet naturalist, in Waterton's famous pejorative phrase.

However, Clare had to use some order in compiling his personal check-list, the greater part of which is included in what follows – the omissions are mainly statements of absence or records of occurrence at second hand. What he did was to use one of the few bird books in his small personal library, the anonymous *Natural History of Birds*, published at Bungay, Suffolk, in 1815. This was in fact a pirated edition of the bird section of Oliver Goldsmith's famous *Animated Nature*, originally published in 1774. So the order used by Clare in his notes was already some fifty years out of date when he wrote. However, we have felt that, all things considered, this is the most appropriate order to use in this selection. It may cause some puzzlement to those used to modern field guides, but this is in no sense a field guide. Rather it is a natural history in the old sense, with the accent as much on the history as on the natural.

We have also used the vernacular names that Clare himself used, indicating, where these differ from current usage, the modern name in square brackets. The Latin scientific name, which will enable non-English speakers to identify the bird more readily, will be found in the index.

NOTE ON THE TEXT

Clare's spelling and punctuation are preserved but we have left spaces between the sentences where Clare left none. We have done this in the belief that the modern reader accustomed to punctuation may be distracted if obliged constantly to retrace his steps in order to find the limits of a sentence. Whenever the reader finds himself in doubt about the meaning of a word he should read it aloud since Clare spelled by ear, and a Northamptonshire ear at that. If that does not suffice the reader should then consult the glossary.

Clare regularly confuses some words – 'where' and 'were', 'than' and 'then', 'lose' and 'loose', 'scare' and 'scar', 'layer' and 'lair' – and tends to misspell words like 'generally', 'numerous', 'domesticated', etc. which were not part of his everyday vocabulary. Other words, however, are genuine dialect variants – 'brun' for 'brown', 'shill' for 'shrill', 'pales' or 'pails' for 'palings', 'newling' for 'a new one', 'pads' for 'paths', etc. Most of these should not create difficulties for the reader once he is accustomed to Clare's mode of speech. On a few occasions we have footnoted a word that might be hard to interpret.

Where the name of a bird has been inserted by the editors as an aid to identification, it appears between square brackets, as do all other editorial additions, including the number of the manuscript and the page from which the extract is taken, given at the end of the passage. Page numbers prefixed with the letter R indicate reverse reading of the manuscript. MSS given the letter N before the number are in Northampton Public Library: all other MSS are from Peterborough Museum. A46, 168 therefore = p. 168 of Peterborough MS A46.

RAPACIOUS BIRDS

Hawks

Hawks are beautiful objects when on the wing   I have often stood to view a hawk [kestrel] in the sky trembling its wings and then hanging quite still for a moment as if it was as light as a shadow and coud find like the clouds a resting place upon the still blue air

They are a great many different sorts of hawks about us and several to which I am a stranger too

There is a very large blue one [Montagu's harrier or hen-harrier] almost as big as a goose they flye in a swopping heavy manner not much unlike the flye of a heron   you may see ann odd one often in the spring swimming close to the green corn and ranging over an whole field for hours together   it hunts leverets Partridges and Pheasants   I saw one of these which a man had wounded with a gun   he had stupified it only for when he got it home it was as fierce as and as live as ever   the wings when extended was of a great length   it was of a blue grey color hued with deeper tinges of the same   its beak was dreadfully hookd and its claws long and of a bright yellow with a yellow ring round each eye which gave a fierce and very severe look   at the sight of a cat it put itself in a posture for striking as if it meant to seize it as prey but at a dog it seemd rather scard and sat on its tail end in a defensive posture with its wings extended and its talons open making at the same time a strange earpiercing hissing noise which dis mayd the dog who woud drop his tail and sneak out as if in fear   they tyd a piece of tar marling to one of its legs and tetherd it in a barn were they kept it 3 or 4 days when it knawd the string from its leg and effected its liberty by getting thro the barn holes in the wall   it ate nothing all that time   they offerd it carrion but it woud take no notice of it   what its name is I know not   they call it the blue hawk

There is a small blue hawk [male sparrow hawk] often mistaken for the cuckoo   I know nothing of it further then seeing it often on the wing and a rare one [merlin] about the size of a black bird of a mottld color with a white patch of feathers on the back of the head one of these sort was shot here this summer by a field keeper   I have never seen any thing like it before*

Last year I had two tame hawks of what species I cannot tell [kestrel]   they was not quite so large as the sparrow hawk   their wings and back feathers was of a red brown color sheathd wi black their tails was long and bard with black and their breasts was a lighter color and spotted   their eyes was large and of a dark piercing blue   their beaks was very much hookd with a sharp projecting swell in the top mandible not unlike the swell in the middle of the hookd bill usd by hedgers and calld by them a tomahawk   this made an incision like a knife in tearing its food   the bottom mandible was curiously shortend as it were for the hook to lap over and seemd as tho nature had clipt the end off with sissors for that purpose   their legs was short and yellow with a tuft of feathers over each thigh like the bantum fowl a property belonging to most of the hawk tribe they grew very tame and woud come at a call or whistle when they was hungry   they made a strange noise that piercd the ear with its shrillness   they was very fond of washing themselves often doing it twice a day in winter   after being fed they woud play in the garden running after each other and seizing bits of clods or fallen apples in their claws or catching at flies   when they rested they usd always to perch on one leg with the other drawn up among their feathers   they always lovd to perch on the top most twig of the trees in the garden were they woud sit in a bold and comanding atitude   one was much larger then the other and the large one was much the tamest   When I went a walking in the fields it woud attempt to flye after me and as I was fearful of loosing it I usd to drive it back but one day it took advantage of watching and following me and when I got into the fields I was astonishd and startld to see a hawk settle on my shoulder   it was mine who had watchd me out of the town and took a short cut to flye after me   I thought it woud flye away for good so I attempted to catch it but it woud not be made a prisoner and flew to the trees by the road side   I gave it up for lost but as soon as I got out of sight it set up a noise and flew after me agen and when I got upon the heath were there was no trees it woud settle upon the ground before me and if I attempted to catch it it woud run and hide in the rabbit burrows and when I left it took wing and flew after me and so

* At the end of this paragraph Clare has the verse-line:
Their very shadow seems to feel a fear

KESTREL

it kept on to the end of my journey when it found home as soon as I did   after this I took no more heed of loosing them tho they woud be missing for days together   a boy caught one by suprise and hurt it so that it dyd and the tamest dyd while I was absent from home 4 days it refusd food and hunted for me every morning and came to sit in my empty chair as it woud do till I got up   they thought it fretted itself to death in my absence but I think the meat I gave was too strong for it and I believd it was not well a good while before I left it   I felt heartily sorry for my poor faithful and affectionat hawk [A46, 116–17]

Falcon Tribe

HAIREY LEGD FALCON [ROUGH-LEGGED BUZZARD]

one shot at a Spring in holly well*   [A46, 163]

OSPREY

one shot by Henderson† in Milton Park – said to build its nest on the ground among reeds with sticks and a lining of flags and to lay 4 white eggs about the size of the hens‡   [A46, 132]

BUZZARD

Is of an idle disposition and not unlike the Kite while perched but quite different when on the wing – it flyes in a flopping manner somthing like the owl and is soon tired and seeks its perch on some old tree were it sits for hours together   it builds a flat nest of sticks lined with old rags and wool somthing like the kites but smaller and very often makes shift with an old crows nest by patching it up and making it a newling   it lays three eggs somthing like the Kites but shorter of a dirty white largly splashd at the large end with blood colored spots and freckled with small ones of a pale red   [A46, 163]

MOOR BUZZARD [MARSH or MONTAGU'S HARRIER]

Haunts the commons about Whittlesea Meer   Scrats a hole on the

---

* Clare's Journal under Sunday 6 Feb. 1825 has the entry: '. . . a bird of the hawk kind was shot at a fountain in hollywell Park of a large size which he [Ned Simpson of Stamford] calls the *"hair legd falcon"*.' [N15, 53]

† Henderson was the gardener at Milton.

‡ A46, 132 has the following note: 'A water bird of the hawk species as large in the body and not unlike a goose with web feet and bill hookd for tearing food   the color all over was a watery white and brown shaded like the breast of the crane shot by Ben Price   it flew heavy like the Kite and I calld it the Sea Hawk   I could not find it in Pennant'

ground and lays 3 eggs of a dirty white color blotchd at the large end
with dun colored spots   [A46, 163]

ASH COLORED BUZZARD [MALE HEN or MONTAGU'S HARRIER]

somthing of this kind flyes over the wheat fields in weeding time and
appears to be hunting its prey   it is said to feed on leverets and
partridges   [A46, 163; *see also p. 1*]

KITE

will bring an thing to their young & when injured   [A46,163]

> . . . Rapt in delight I often stood
> Gazing on scenes that seemd to smile
> And oft to view for field and wood
> I clomb a neighbouring stile
> Were saild the puddock still and proud
> Assaild at first by swopping crows
> But soon it met the morning cloud
> And scornd such humble foes
>
>   [A23, 36]

                    *   *   *

> The sailing puddock sweeps about for prey
> And keeps above the woods from day to day
> They make a nest so large in woods remote
> Would fill a womans apron with the sprotes
> And schoolboys daring doing tasks the best
> Will often climb and stand upon the nest
> They find a hugh old tree and free from snaggs
> And make a flat nest lined with wool and rags
> And almost big enough to make a bed
> And lay three eggs and spotted oer with red
> The schoolboy often hears the old ones cry
> And climbs the tree and gets them ere they fly
> And takes them home and often cuts their wing
> And ties them in the garden with a string
>
>   [B9, 71]

GOSHAWK

haunts the heaths about holy well and appears to hide among the
furze   [A46, 163]

SPARROW HAWK

[*See p. 1*]   [A46, 163]

KESTREL

said to be the species that hangs in the air on trembling wings and is a
beautiful object in the blue sky of a summers day

[A46, 163; *see pp. 1–2*]

HOBBY

this was the species that I kept tame [*but see pp. 2–4*]   [A46, 163]

MIRLIN [MERLIN]

a hawk of passage   [A46, 163; *see p. 1*]

Owl Tribe

OWLS

'The moping owl that to the moon complains' is not destitute of
beautys to the Poets rambles   its solitary note of 'Tewit [? tewho'] is
often ecchod in the songs of the bard   shakspear calls it a 'merry
note'   tis hard to call his taste into question but I really must confess
my ignorance that I cannot find a reason why he makes it so   it
sounds in my ear always as it did in Grays a note that bespoke
complaining sadness rather then merriment   there are 4 sorts with
us the barn or wheaten owl the large wood owl and small owl [tawny
owl] and the short horned owl [long-eared owl] 3 of which was shot
by Artis* in Milton Park   the barn owl watches for mice on the
mows builds a nest of straws and sticks in a hole on† the top of the
side wall and lays 6 eggs of a dirty white and largly patchd with spots
of a dark red or blood color   the other sorts build in hollows on the
heads of dotterels lays generally 6 eggs of a lighter color then the
barn owl   they are very fierce when they have young and attack the
boys when they climb their nests in such a fierce fearless manner as
often drives the robbers down and save their young   when a boy I
have witnessd this myself   there was an old tree in a thicket call[d]
western close spinney which had an owls nest in it yearly   in one of

* Artis was the Steward of the Fitzwilliam estates and a distinguished amateur
classical archaeologist.
† Clare repeats 'on'.

my attempts to rob it the owl attackted me in so fierce a manner that I
believd it to be no other then a witch in the shape of an owl and I fell*
from the tree and never after attempted to rob it agen   the young
are coverd with a white down like chickens and when nearly fledgd
they fling themselves in a devensive posture on their backs and make
a noise with their beaks which I usd to compare to cracking nutts
woodpigens will do somthing in the same manner when young
they do not seize their prey by night as is commonly gave out but just
at sun set when one may hear the little birds loud and clamorous in
their calls of danger were ever the owl approaches   [A46, 125]

HORNED OWL [LONG-EARED OWL]
said to build in the old hollow thorn trees in Milton park

[A46, 163; *see above*]

BARN OWL

SCREECH OWL [BARN OWL]
lays in the holes of barn walls 6 eggs of a white colour largly blotcht
with spots of a blood red   screeches – preys on small birds and
mice   often flyes out in the day time in dull weather and autumn

[A46, 163; *see above*]

* Clare has written 'feel'.

BROWN OWL OR SMALL HOOP OWL [TAWNY OWL]

frequents woods and hedge borders builds in hollow trees lays 5 eggs
much like the other   feeds on small birds   [A46, 163]

LARGE WOOD OWLE [TAWNY OWL]

the boldest of the Owl tribe builds in hollow trees in woods and
thicketts feeds on young rabbits leverets and birds   atacks boys in a
bold manner who ventures to take its nest   account of one in Bulls
spinney   [A46, 163]

Butcher bird* Tribe

WOOD CHAT [RED-BACKED SHRIKE]

frequents woods builds a nest of bents and hairiff lined with small
fibres of roots and horsehair lays 5 eggs of a dun or fox brown color
mark[d] with cloudy spots of deeper hue   genrearly builds in the
thick squatty bushes of the wood briar   [A46, 163]

* Clare has written 'bride'.

BIRDS OF THE PIE KIND

Crow Tribe

RAVEN

account of a tame one   builds on large trees whose bodys are
destitute of branches and difficult to climb   it is a large nest built in
the collar of the tree which tree they keep as there annual home for
many years   its eggs are olive green blotchd with bluish grey and
liver colored spots   do great damage to sheep in the fens   [A46, 163]

a pair had a nest on a larg ash tree in etton field hedge for 10 or 12
years and when that was cut down the same or a pair of the family
occupyd a large inaccessable oak in Oxey wood which they occupy
still   [A46, 164]

> And sooty raven in the winter warm
> That plays and tumbles in the pelting storm
> [A49, 37]

CROW [CARRION CROW]

The Crow

How peaceable it seems for lonely men
To see a crow fly in the thin blue sky
Over the woods and fealds, o'er level fen
It speaks of villages, or cottage nigh
Behind the neighbouring woods – when march winds high
Tear off the branches of the hugh old oak
I love to see these chimney sweeps sail by
And hear them o'er the knarled forest croak
Then sosh askew from the hid woodmans stroke
That in the woods their daily labours ply
I love the sooty crow nor would provoke
Its march day exercises of croaking joy
I love to see it sailing to and fro
While feelds, and woods and waters spread below
[20(i), 216]

9

BLUE FEN CROW/ROYSTON CROW [HOODED CROW]

The blue Crow builds on thorn bushes in the fens – seldom venturing
on trees   its eggs are similar to common Crows but of a paler colour
and slenderer in shape   [A49, 74]

> The dreary fen a waste of water goes
> With nothing to be seen but royston crows
>   [A61, 41]

ROOK

> The rooks begin to build and pleasant looks
> The homestead elms now almost black with rooks
> The birds at first for mastership will try
> They fight for sticks and squabble as they flye
> And if a stranger comes they soon invade
> And pull his nest in pieces soon as made
> The carrion crow and hawk dare never come
> They dare to fight like armys round their home
> The boughs will hardly bear their noisey guests
> And storms will come and over turn the nests
> They build above the reach of clauming crows
> They climb and feel but cunning cuts them down
> Others with reaching poles the nest destroys
> While off and up they flye with deafening noise
>   [B9, 78]

JACKDAW

builds in hollow trees and in the chimneys of uninhabited houses also
in the steeples of churches and they are sed to occupy the holes of
rabbits in some places   they lay 5 or 6 eggs of a pale blue color
speckled with small black spots   [A46, 164]

MAGPIE

build on the highest branches of trees and in the thickest bushes
makes a covering oer its nest with two entrances one* facing the west
and the other the east makes the outside of rough thorny twigs and
lines it with fibres of roots and twitch lays from 5 to 8 eggs of a
watery green color thickly freckled with brown spots   easily tamed

* Clare has 'once'.

MAGPIE

and learnd to talk   I kept one for years till it got drownd in a well
it usd to see its self in the water   I fancy it got down thinking to meet
it*   it used to run away with the tea spoons or any thing which it
coud come at and woud watch its oppertunity as cunningly as a
reasoning being and the moment it found† it was not observed it
woud seize the thing it wanted and hasten out of the house to hide it
in the garden were it woud let it lye a few days and then bring it in
again – it imitated many words readily and when it heard a sound or
word that it coud not imitate readily it woud become silent and
pensive and sit ruminating on an eldern tree and muttering as it were
to itself som inaudible sounds till at length it got by heart the thing it
was aiming at and then it was as lively and as full of chatter as ever

[A46, 164]

Magpies have always two openings into their nest one to enter
into it and one to escape from it – I have often got my hand into the
nest before the old one has left it when she has sat hard on her eggs
and she always escaped at another hole
    Magpies always line their nests with twitch and dried roots –
Crows use twitch roots old rags and wool –- but the magpie never
uses wool or any thing but roots and twitch
    Jaybirds uses dead roots and twitch like the magpie but they are
generally of finer texture   [A49, 74]

> . . . and yonder by the circling stack
> Provoking any eye to smile
> A pye perched on the heifers back
> Pulls hair to line her nest the while
> That winds upon the high oak rocks
> The threat of every storm
> Yet still it stands the rudest shocks
> A sweeing cradle snug and warm
>
> [A57, 52]

JAY

this is a beautiful‡ bird from the fine blue patch on each wing   it
builds on the sides of trees in woods and in bushes in thicketts

* Clare presumably intended to write 'itself'.
† Clare has 'fond'.
‡ Clare has 'beautif'.

commonly chusing the white thorn   it makes the outside of its nest
with stick and lines it with twitch and small fiberes of roots   it lays 5
and 6 eggs of a pale greenish color thickly mozzled with small
brunny spots – it is a sort of pilot among the birds and warns them by
a harsh noise not unlike a childs rattle of danger   [A46, 164]

> The jay set up his copple crown
> And screamed to see a stranger
> And swopt and hurried up and down
> To warn the birds of danger
> And magpies where the spinney was
> Noised five and six together
> While patiently the woodmans ass
> Stood stretching round his tether
>
> [A59, 71]

*　　*　　*

> . . . and often from the nestling sun
> The jay bird calls and starts away
> A warning to the birds around
> That peeping dangers on the way
> The blackbird answers and the rest
> Start silent from each mossy nest
>
> [A57, 3]

Cuckoo Tribe

CUCKOO

Gordons tale of one laying in a wagtails nest   generaly prefers a
eith* a wagtails or a hedge sparrows drops no more then one egg in a
nest   it is† a short one of a beatiful blush color clouded at the large
end with a deeper hue   they are small and not much larger then the
hedge sparrows – after singing times it preys on young birds and is
often mistaken for the hawk whose character in many [ways]‡ it
asumes – the young cuckoos are said to be hollow backd and throw
out the young ones that are hatchd with them – some people say that
they are hollow backd and that by contriving to get the young

* Clare seems to have intended to write 'either' but forgot to delete 'a'.
† Clare has omitted 'is'.
‡ There is a space in the MS here.

sparrow theron they throw him overboard but* I have not been able to observe this and cannot assertain the truth of it

[A46, 164; *see also pp. 33, 48–9,* HEDGE SPARROW]

[*Natural History Letter III*] . . . As to the cuckoo I can give you no further tidings than† what I have given in my last   Artis has one in his collection of stuffd birds but I have not the sufficient scientific curosity about me to go and take the exact description of its head rump and wings the length of its tail and the breadth from the tips of the extended wings   these old bookish descriptions you may find in any natural history if they are of any gratification   for my part I love to look on nature with a poetic feeling which magnifys the pleasure   I love to see the nightingale in its hazel retreat and the cuckoo hiding in its solitudes of oaken foliage and not to examine their carcasses in glass cases . . .   [A49, 44]

The Cuckoo

The cuckoo like a hawk in flight
With narrow pointed wings
Wews oer our heads – soon out of sight
And as she flies she sings
And darting down the hedge row side
She scar[e]s the little bird
Who leaves the nest it cannot hide
While plaintive notes are heard

Ive watched it on an old oak tree
Sing half an hour away
Untill its quick eye noticed me
And then it whewed away
Its mouth when open shone as red
As hips upon the briar
Like stock doves seemed its wings and head
But striving to get nigher

It heard me and above the trees
Soon did its flight pursue
Still waking summers melodies
And singing as it flew

* Clare has 'by'.   † Clare has 'that'.

So quick it flies from wood to wood
Tis miles off ere you think it gone
Ive thought when I have listening stood
Full twenty sang – when only one

When summer from the forrest starts
Its melody with silence lies
And like a bird from foreign parts
It cannot sing for all it tries
'Cuck cuck' it cries and mocking boys
Crie 'Cuck' and then it stutters more
Till quite forgot its own sweet voice
It seems to know itself no more

Wryneck Tribe

WRYNECK

a beautiful bird of different shades of brown whose various shades is
not observable till close to it   when it sits on its nest or on a tree it
makes an odd motion with its head turning about first to the left and
then the right and I think this motion gave it the name of Ryneck   it
builds in hollow trees and in the old deserted holes of Wood-
peckers   it is a bird of passage and comes a few days before the
firetail   it has a very long tongue like the Woodpecker and appears
to be of that tribe feeding on insects tho it appears unable to make
any use of its bill in the boreing of holes &c and it makes its nest of
moss and dead grass lined with cobwebs and other light materials
it lays a large quantity of eggs   I have my self found nests with 16 in
them often   they are a little larger then those of the sparrow and are
of a delicate snowey white with out spot or stain   the circle at the
end calld the tread may be distinctly seen – I found one last year in
Billings Orchard with 16 eggs in it – I took 6 out and she sat on the
rest and raisd the young ones – when one approachd the nest the old
one made a hissing noise and turnd her head in an odd motion from
side to side   [A46, 164]

GREEN WOOD PECKER

a beautiful bird very common bores holes in the hard trees were it
makes its nest of moss and a lining of hair and wool   it lays 5 eggs
about the size of the sparrows and not much unlike them tho more

thickly spotted with small dark spots – its flight is an easy motion of ups and downs fluttering its wings at every rise and closing them motionless at every fall   it may be heard boring its hole at the beginning of spring making an odd cranking sound like a carpenter turning his wimble in hard wood   it taps at the side of trees very often as if it tryd by the sound to see if they were hollow but perhaps its real purpose is to search for Insects   it bores for the larve of Moths and butterflys in rottend trees and old gate posts   it is a very solitary bird rarely being seen with its own species even in breeding time   [A46, 165]

[*Natural History Letter IX*]   [25 March 1825]
. . . have you never heard that cronking jaring noise in the woods at this early season   I heard it to day and went into the woods to examine what thing it was that caused the sound and I discoverd that it was the common green woodpecker busily employd at boreing his hole which he effected by twisting his bill round in the way that a carpenter twists his wimble with this difference that when he has got it to a certain extent he turns it back and then pecks awhile and then twists agen   his beak seems to serve all the purposes of a nail passer gough and wimble effectually   what endless new lessons may we learn from nature . . .   [A49, 69]

> The green woodpecker flying up and down
> With wings of mellow green and speckled crown
> She bores a hole in trees with crawking noise
> And pelted down and often catched by boys
> She makes a lither nest of grass and whool
> Men fright her oft that go the sticks to pull
> And stood on rotten grains to reach the hole
> And as I trembled upon fear and doubt
> I found the eggs and scarce could get them out
> I put them in my hat a tattered crown
> And scarsely without breaking brought them down
> The eggs are small for such a bird they lay
> Five eggs and like the sparrows spotted grey
>   [B9, 69]

GREAT SPOTTED WOODPECKER

this is smaller then the green one tho its habits are the same   it is of a pied color of brown and white with a red crown and a dingy hue of red on the under parts of the belly – it taps more frequently on the trees then the green one but is not so often seen as it generally keeps about the tops of the trees and makes the hole for its nest in the grains   I know nothing of its eggs as I never have had as yet the good fortune to meet with a nest – it seems to have a quick ear at the approach of any thing from which it seldom flyes but nimbles on the other side of the grain out of sight – there is a smaller one of the same color as this [lesser spotted woodpecker] but not so common   I have seen it often but know nothing of its habits any way different from the former   [A46, 165]

GREAT SPOTTED WOODPECKER

When Woodpeckers are making or boring their holes in the spring they are so attentive over their labours that they are easily caught by boys who watch them when they are half hid in the holes they are making and climbing softly up the tree make them prisoners – a* nest thus left unfinished is never resumed by another – the male

* Clare has 'as'.

17

makes the holes generally and when finished sets up a continued cry
to invite a companion that seldom fails to join him in seeking
materials for lining the nest – the pied woodpecker never bores holes
in the body of the tree but in the larger grains very high up and
always on the underneath side so that they are inaccesable to nest
hunting boys – it is easy to see where this tribe are making new nests
by the litter they make at the foot of the tree as if it where sawdust

[A49, 84]

There is a small woodpecker red and grey
That hides in woods and forrests far away
They run like creepers up and down the tree
And few can find them when they stand to see
They seldom fly away but run and climb
A man may stand and look for twenty time
And seldom see them once for half a day
Ive stood nor seen them till they flew away
Ive swarmed the grain and clumb with hook and pole
But scarce could get three fingers in the hole
They build on grains scarse thicker then ones legs
Ive found the nests but never got the eggs
But boys who wish to see what eggs they lay
Will climb the tree and saw the grain away

[B9, 69]

Nuthatch Tribe

NUTHATCH

of a beautiful color not unlike the blue titmouse but larger runs
about trees like the woodpecker and is seldom seen as it haunts
solitary places   I have never found its nest but I shoud expect that it
builds in trees   there are tales of its being able to crack nuts but I can
say nothing for its authenticity   [A46, 165]

In summer showers a skreeking noise is heard
Deep in the woods of some uncommon bird
It makes a loud and long and loud continued noise
And often stops the speed of men and boys
They think somebody mocks and goes along
And never thinks the nuthatch makes the song

Who always comes along the summers guest
But bird nest hunters never found the nest
The schoolboy hears the noise from day to day
And stoops among the thorns to find a way
And starts the jay bird from the bushes green
He looks and sees a nest he's never seen
And takes the spotted eggs with many joys
And thinks he found the bird that made the noise

[B9, 98]

Kingfisher Tribe

KING FISHER

its plumage of glossy orange green and blue is very beautiful   in
shape it resembles the wood pecker – it feeds on fish and sits on a
branch of a tree that hangs over a river for hours on the watch for any
small fish that passes bye when it darts down and seizes its prey in a
moment – they make there nests in holes on banks sides by the
water   they lay 5 and sometimes 6 eggs of a milk white color   they
make no nest but lay them on the bareground tho quantitys of fishes
bones placed in a curious manner like a nest are found in the holes
after the birds are flown   I have heard fisher men say that they are
the bones of the fish on which the young ones are fed – in some places
they hand a dead king fisher up the kitchen to note the weather by as
it is said that its head turns to the rainy quarter when ever rain is
expected   there is a larger bird of a pied color much like the former
in shape and habits very common about the fen dykes which the
inhabitants call a kingfisher*   it flyes on the top of the water down
rivers and dykes and often siezes its prey on the wing – it makes its
nest on the ground in the reed beds and lays 5 large eggs of a dirty
brown colour   the young take the water as soon as hatchd [A46,165]

In coat of orange green and blue
Now on a willow branch I view
Grey waving to the sunny gleam
King fishers watch the ripple stream
For little fish that nimble bye
And in the gravel shallows lie

* Clare has 'kingfishers'.

KINGFISHER

Creeper Tribe

CREEPER [TREE CREEPER]

common with us runs up the sides of trees like the wood pecker very small and of a light brown color   it builds in hollow willows and in the deserted holes of woodpeckers lays 8 or 9 small white eggs spotted with feint red spots   it is calld by the wood men the treecreeper and by some the willow biter as it makes incisions in the last years twigs of willows for some insects deposited in them

[A46, 165]

PASSERINE BIRDS

Starling Tribe

STARLING

they are curiously mottled with white specks all about their dark
feathers   they build early in spring and lay in hollow trees and in
chimneys of uninhabtied house also in old walls   their eggs are of a
greenish blue speckled with small spots   they are easily made tame
and learn to whistle tunes and talk words and even speak short
sentences with great [   ] a Gipsey in the Smiths gang had one
that was so tame that it needed no cage to confine it   in Autumn
they collect together in large flocks and may be heard* making a loud
chattering on commons and in closes were they settle to feed   they
like to pick somthing out of horse dung – in the evening the go in
large flocks to roost and may be heard wirling along in the dusky
sky   they perch in the reed shaws on whittlesea meer and do great
damage to the reed† by bending it down with their numbers and the
reed cutters often stand knocking them with large poles to keep them
from settling – it is said that they do hurt to dove‡ coats and suck the
eggs of the piegons but this is a falshood a [   ]   [A46, 166]

> The starnel builds in chimneys from the view
> And lays a egg like thrushes paley blue
> Then breeds and flyes and in the closes dwells
> Where new made haystacks yield a pleasant smell
> [B9, 60]

Thrush Tribe

BLACK BIRD

a pert bird builds its nest in hedges and thickets of dead grass and
moss without side and adds a lair of cow dung and lines it with grass

---

* Clare has 'heart'.   † Clare has 'read'.   ‡ Clare has 'doe'.

BLACKBIRD

of finer sorts now and then inserting a few oak leaves   it lays 5 eggs
of greenish ash color thickly freckeld with brunny spots   it feeds on
shell snails in winter and dexterously breaks them agen a stone or
any hard substance that it can find the readiest   the blackbird has
often* been said to sing in winter   it does some times in very open
weather but very rarely and the song of the Mavis thrush is often
mistaken for that of the blackbird which has created this common
mistake   [A46, 166]

January 25 [? 1811] – Heard the blackbird singing in Royce Wood as
earnest as if it was April   [A48, R43; *see also pp. 33–5,* HOUSE SPARROW]

    Blackbirds and Thrushes particularly the former feed in hard
winters upon the shell snail horns by hunting them from the hedge
bottoms and wood stulps and taking them to a stone where they
brake them in a very dexterous manner – any curious observer of
nature may see in hard frosts the shells of pootys thickly litterd round
a stone in the lanes and if he waits a short time he will quickly see one
of these birds coming with a snailhorn in his bill which he constantly
taps on the stone till it is broken   he then extracts the snail and like a
true sportsman eagerly hastens to hunt them again in the hedges or
woods where a frequent rustle of their little feet is heard among the
dead leaves   [A49, 82]

> The blackbird
> Rustling in the hedge bottoms for
> falling wild fruit is often scared from his meal
> by the slim weazel bobbing from hollow roots
>   [A18, 205]

*   *   *

> . . . That blackbirds music from the hazel bower
> Turns into golden drops this summer shower
> To think the rain that wets his sutty wing
> Should wake the gushes of his soul to sing
> Hark at the melody how rich and loud
> Like daylight breaking through the morning cloud
> How luscious through that sea of green it floats

* Clare has 'of'.

Knowest thou of music breathed from sweeter
  notes
Than that wild minstrel of the summer shower
Breathes at this moment from that hazel bower
To me the anthem of a thousand tongues
Were poor and idle to the simple songs
To that high toned and edifying bird
That sings to nature by itself unheard . . .

[A49, 37]

*   *   *

The cloudy morning brought a pleasant day
And soon the busy mist was all away
When forth I wandered out and chanched to see
A woodbine twining round a stoven tree
That ventured up and formed a bush at top
And bended leaning till it met a prop
And overhung with leaves so thick a shade
You couldnt see the nest the black bird made
Who fluttered oer my head as if from boys
And soon her partner answered to the noise
The path went closely bye but seldom prest
By passer bye who never saw the nest
The old birds sat and sung in safety sure
And the young brood pin feathered lay secure

[A61, 81]

*   *   *

The blackbird closely sits upon her nest
To hide her young brood from the rainy day

[A57, 10]

MISSEL THRUSH [MISTLE THRUSH]

[*Natural History Letter V*] . . . I find more beautys in this month
[February] then I can find room to talk about in a letter and particu-
lary as you prefer the living objects to the landscape – In this month
the Mavis thrush begins to build its nest   it is about as large as the
field fare and not much unlike it   its song is very stunt and unvaried
and seems like the song of a young bird while learning to sing but the

season at which it sings always makes it welcome and beautiful for it begins very early and if its a open Winter it may be heard at the end of December and beginning of January   it loves to frequent at this season old orchards and hedge borders in home-steads near the village when it can get shelter and cover as if it loved to treat the village with a song at such a dreary season   as the spring advances its song ceases and it disappears to its more solitary haunts of woods and forrests were it generaly builds its nest beside a large tree on the twigs and water grains that shoot from the body   its nest is made of the blades of dead grass moss and cow dung lined with warmer materials of wool and a finer sort of grass intermixd   it often lays six eggs much like the black birds but larger of of a deeper blue green dusted with brun colored spots   its nest has been often mistaken for the black birds but it is easily distinguishd by the more curious observer as the blackbird uses moss on the out side and lines the inside with fine twitchy roots and hair while the mavis never forgets her dead ramping grass for the outside covering and a plentiful supply of wool within   the wool is what bird nesting boys know it bye   [A49, 51]

FIELD FARE

saw one last sunday 17 April   they come in large flocks and strip the awe bushes as they proceed onward in their march   they stay later some years then others but generaly leave in the begining of April   they are speckled like the thrush and make* a busy chinnying as they flye   [A46, 166]

1829 Saw a nest formed like the blackbirds on the tiptop of the old Elm in Bradfords yard   I thought they were field fares   they were of the thrush kind and made a strange chattering noise when they left it in the morning as they flew but were silent all the day and I never could observe them come to feed their young all the day tho I watchd them narrowly – I still fancy they were the field fare   [A49, 86]

SINGING THRUSH/THROSTLE THRUSH [SONG THRUSH]

[*Natural History Letter V*] . . . the Thrush celebrated for its fine song is a small bird not much larger then a groundlark   it does not begin its varied song till May which is said by some to equal the nightin-

* Clare repeats 'and make'.

gales which it very much resembles tho it is not so various   it builds
its nest about the latter end of april and makes the out side of green
moss and lines the inside with touch wood from decayd trees and
cowdung which it plasters round in a very workman like manner and
makes it as round as the spoon of a Ladle that dryes as hard as brick
after it is finished   tho this may be thought to be a hard bed for its
young it uses no other lining   it lays 5 and some times six eggs
smaller then the black birds of a beautiful blue like the hedge-
sparrows but thinly mottled at the large end with inky spots   it

SONG THRUSH

mostly nay I might say always chuses the white thorn to build on and
seeks the most retired places of the wood seldom venturing to hazard
its nest in the hedge or near the side   I have often remarkd an odd
scircumstance respecting these birds in laying time which I never
coud account for which is the frequent desertion of their nests after
they were finished not only of one but of 19 out of twenty as if
the birds had by a natural impulse joind their minds to leave their
new made dwellings and migrate to other countys   this does not
appear to be the case every season but when it is so it seems to be

general   the year before last I found 12 nests in Oxey wood all left in this manner as if they all left off at the same instant   it was before the cuckoo had made* her appearance or I should have laid the blame to her   when this general desertion takes place the nests are always more numeros then at other times − but there are a many of natures riddles not yet resolved −. . .   [A49, 52]

RED WING −

smaller then the field fare not so numerous   flyes silent   [A46, 166]

Grosbeak Tribe

GROSS BEAK [HAWFINCH]

seen here − Artis   [A46, 166]

GREEN LINNET [GREENFINCH]

builds in thorn bushes makes a rather clumsey nest of moss and dead airiff stalks and wool lined† with cow hair and wool lays five eggs longish of a white color faintly spotted with red and purple spots at the large end   [A46, 166]

BULLFINCH

[*Natural History Letter IV*] . . . − the Bullfinch is a beautiful bird   the plumage is fine and its shape tho rather heavy is commanding and noble   it begins to build in may   its nest is an odd curious one nearly flat made in a negligent manner of small sticks and lined with morsels of fine twitch and roots   it generally builds in a thick clump of Briars or black thorn   its eggs are about as large as the hedgesparrows of a greenish or watery white freckled at the thick end with pale lilac and dark brown spots not much unlike the green linnets   its song is rather varied and pretty   it is a great destroyer of the buds of fruit trees in winter like the black and blue Tit-mouse and its fine plumage and pretty song cannot make any petition for its crime to the enraged gardiner who shoots it with the others indiscriminatly − in winter it frequents gardens and orchards and in spring it returns to its wild solitudes of woods and commons were it can feed in saftey . . .   [A49, 47]

* Clare has written 'mader'.
† Clare has 'lineed'.

Bunting Tribe

BUNTING LARK [CORN BUNTING]

calld ground Lark here has no song may be seen twittering its wings
on the top twigs of bushes and uttering a small 'cree creeing' noise –
it is very like the lark but larger – they build on the ground in the
meadow grass or wheat fields   they make a nest in an hole or
horsefooting of straw and dead grass lined with twitchy fibres and
horsehair and lay 5 and some times six dirty colored eggs markd with
a purple tinge round the large end   [A46, 166]

> Close where the milking maidens pass
> In roots and twitches drest
> Within a little bunch of grass
> A groundlark made her nest
> The maiden touched her with her gown
> And often frit her out
> And looked and set her buckets down
> But never found it out
> The eggs where large and spotted round
> And dark as is the fallow ground
> The schoolboy kicked the grass in play
> But danger never guest
> And when they came to mow the hay
> They found an empty nest
>
> [B9, 72]

YELLOW HAMMER

a bold bird builds its nest on the ground and in low bushes of dead
grass and twitch and lines it with horse hair lays five eggs of a fleshy
ash color streaked all over with black crooked lines as if done with a
pen and for this it is often called the 'writing lark' and thought by
birdnesting boys to be a different bird from the yellow hamer   it
likes to build in banks facing the sun by dykes &c   [A46, 167]

May 2nd   My Boys found a yellowhammers nest with 5 eggs in it in
a goosberry bush – they frequently build on the ground under a
molehill or bank by a brook – and a mavis thrushes nest under some
faggots and a hedge sparrows in the eldens and all not fifty yards
from the house   [A58, 11]

YELLOWHAMMER

Fixed in a white thorn Bush its summer guest
Sow low een grass oer topt its tallest twig
A yellow hammer built its twitchy nest
Close by the brook bank and the wooden brig
Where school boys every morn and eve did pass
In robbing birds and cunning deeply skilled
Searching each bush and taller clumps of grass
Where ere was liklihood of birds to build
Yet did she heir her habitation long
And keep her little brood from dangers eye
Hidden as secret as a crickets song
Till they on well fledged pinions swept the sky
Proving that providence is often bye
To guard the simplest of her charge from wrong

[N17, 131]

*   *   *

the hare
Cheat of its chosen bed and from the bank
The yellow hammer flutter in short fears
From of its nest hid in the grasses rank
And drops again when no more noise it hears

[N17, 123]

*   *   *

The yellow hammer never makes a noise
But flyes in silence from the noisey boys
The boys will come and take them every day
And still she lays as none were taen away

[A61, 8]

REED SPARROW [REED BUNTING]

It is a brown slender bird with a black head and has some resem-
blance to the sparrow   it haunts lakes and marshy places and builds
a curious nest among the dead reed or on the bank by the side of the
water always choosing a place that is difficult to be come at   its nest
is made of dead grass and always lined with the down of the reed   it
lays 5 and some times six eggs not much unlike the white throats but
larger of a dirty white freckled with brown and purple spots at the

31

large end   they are solitary birds and are seldom seen more then two
together   they have a sort of Song but not fine or varied

[A46, 167; *see also p. 33*]

Finch Tribe

SPARROWS

3 sorts

The common house Sparrow The hedge Sparrow and Reed
Sparrow often calld the fen Sparrow

The common sparrow is well known but not so much so in a
domestacated state as few people think it worth while bringing up a
sparrow   when I was a boy I kept a tamed cock sparrow 3 years   it
was so tame that it woud come when calld and flew were it pleasd
when I first had the sparrow I was fearful of the cats killing it so I usd
to hold the bird in my hand towards her and when she attempted to
smell of it I beat her   she at last woud take no notice of it and I
venturd to let it loose in the house   they were both very shoy at each
other at first and when the sparrow venturd to chirp the cat woud
brighten up as if she intended to seize it but she went no further then
a look or smell   at length she had kittens and when they were taken
away she grew so fond of the sparrow as to attempt to caress it   the
sparrow was startld at first but came too by degrees and venturd so
far at last to perch upon her back   Puss woud call for it when out of
her sight like a kitten and woud lay mice before it the same as she
woud for her own young   they always livd in harmony ever after so
much so that the sparrow woud often take away bits of bread from
under the cats nose and even put itself in a posture for resistance
when offended as if it recond her* nothing more then one of its kind
and in winter when we coud not bear the doors open to let the
sparrow come out and in I was alowd to take a pane out of the
winter† but in the spring of the third year my poor tom sparrow for
that was the name he was calld bye went out and never returnd   I
went day after day‡ calling out for tom and eagerly eying every
sparrow on the house but none answerd the name for he woud come
down in a moment to the call and perch upon my hand to be fed   I
gave it out that some cat which it mistook for its old favourite
betrayd its confidence and destroyd it   [A46, 115]

---

* Clare has 'he'.   † Clare obviously intended to write 'window'.
‡ Clare has 'dy'.

The hedge sparrow builds in hedges and in evergreen shrubs in gardens   it lays five eggs of a beautiful blue color   [A46, 115]

The reed sparrow [reed bunting] builds by the sides of rivers and dykes   it has a black head and rather resembles the cock house sparrow but at a nearer view it is a more slender bird   it makes a nest sometimes on the dyke bank and sometimes among the last years witherd reed   it lays 6 eggs spotted verry much like a white throats but larger and of a different appearence   [A46, 115]

HOUSE SPARROW

build a nest on the thatch under the eaves and at the gable ends in every barn and cottage   its out side is coarsley made of hay and straw but it is painfuly lined with swarms of feathers   I have always observed as far as it came under my observation that those birds whose young leave the shell bare without down always provide for their nakedness in making the nest warm with linings of soft materials as wool and feathers while the others less careful for their offspring while nature provides them with a downy covering line theirs with rooty fibers or horsehair – the sparrow will breed in the hollows of willow trees and often where corn is plenty and houses are scarce on the branches of trees   its nest then is a very large one roughly made of straws and hay as large as ones hat lined warmly with feathers   it is in the form of a bag and the hole or entrance is on one side like the Wrens – I observed several nests the year before last on the elm trees agen our garden (now cut down) were they bred their young   to me it was a very novel appearance to see sparrows nests in so odd a situation   tho I had heard that they woud build on trees I never believed it till then – I believe the reason of their choosing such an odd place to build their houses was the frequent robberys that was made on their homes in the cottage below were a nest never escaped their pilfering   tho I always denied their intrusions on my part of the house yet they woud watch oppertunitys and take them at night after I was in bed – I always thought* it a very cruel practice for the overseers of the parish to give rewards to boys to kill sparrows as they often do it very cruelly and cheat the overseers ignorance a many times in taking other harmless birds to pass them for sparrows to get the bounty – white sparrow seen at Glinton last year   [A46, 167]

* Clare has written 'thuogh'.

HOUSE SPARROW

song birds particularly the Sparrow and Blackbird are very particular in keeping their nests clean taking out the dung and carring it to a good distance from the nest and I have observed also that they pick up the dirt about the ground and carry it away likewise I think this is to keep their nest conseald as where ever* is the boys expect that there is young   [A46, 162]

MOUNTAIN SPARROW [TREE SPARROW]

I think this is our tree Sparrow they are like the house sparrow but smaller yet the never come into the village and in winter I never see them   [A46, 167]

Henderson saw a pair of the tree sparrows agen open wood they are very like the house sparrows but smaller they build in old willow trees and make a nest and lay eggs very like the others but they never haunt villages   [A46, 162]

CHAFFINCH

they are calld 'Pinks' here from the note . . . in winter I have observed that the hen birds are more numerous then the males   [A46, 167]

> The schoolboys in the morning soon as drest
> Went round the fields to play and look for nests
> They found a crows but dare not climb so high
> And looked for nests when any bird was nigh
> At length they got agen a bush to play
> And found a pinks nest round and mossed with grey
> And lined about with feathers and with hair
> They tryed to climb but brambles said forbear
> One found a stone and stronger then the rest
> And took another up to reach the nest
> Heres eggs they hollowed with a hearty shout
> Small round and blotched they reached and tore them out
> The old birds sat and hollowed pink pink pink
> And cattle hurried to the pond to drink
>
>   [B9, 62]

GOLD FINCH OR REDCAP

[*Natural History Letter IV*] . . . The gold finch is well known its song and beautiful plumage like the fair face of womoan proves its

* Clare has 'were ever'.

35

enemey and is the cause of making it a prisoner for life   it is among
the most frequent and commonest of cage birds   it builds its nest
on the eldern or apple tree and makes its outside of grey moss like
the pinks which it greatly resembles but its lining is different and
instead of cowhair it prefers thistle down   it lays 5 pale eggs thinly
sprinkled with feint red spots   in spring it pleasures the cottager
with its song beside his door in the eldern tree and apple by the
orchard pails   it feeds in summer on the groundsel seed and the
broad leafd plantain   when it has raisd its family they all live
happily together parents and childern till the next spring and may be
seen in such companys in winter tracing the common and the fallow
fields were the thistles are in plenty on the seed of which it feeds till
summer returns with its other food – it is not uncommon while
walking down a green lane in early spring to see it perched on the top
of a thistle picking out the seed or pulling the soft down for its nest
and flying into the neighbouring hedge at the approach of a passer-
bye   [A49, 47]

> the red cap too the while
> With gold freckd wings resumes his yearly toil
> And thoughtless were the thieving boys may come
> In the low eldern builds his dangerd home
>
> [A21, 14]

BROWN LINNET [LINNET]

brown linnet or furze linnet builds in furze bushes on heaths makes a
nest of dead grass lined with rabbit fur   lays 5 eggs somthing like the
former but smaller sprinkled with red and purple spots at the large
end – great destroyers of turnip seed of which they are very fond and
it will attract them for miles   their song is beautiful   they are often
called furze larks by the bird catchers and are eroniosly considerd as
different birds   the cock bird has a beautiful flush of red on its
breast   [A46, 166]

LITTLE REDPOLE [LESSER REDPOLL]

I think this is our Goss lark or Red headed linnet –   [A46, 168]

Saw a red headed linnet on Caistor old field   is* like the brown or
Goss linnet but smaller   [A46, 162]

* Clare repeats 'is'.

36

Lark Tribe

LARKS

We have 4 larks here the skye lark the ground lark [corn bunting] the furze lark and the wood lark [tree pipit]

The sky lark is a slender light bird with a coppld crown on the head builds its nest on the ground and lays five or six spotted eggs this is the one celebrated by poets for the sweetness of its song they gather in flocks after harvest and are caught in some parts by nets thrown at night in great quantitys

Cunningham*

The Ground lark [corn bunting] is a much larger bird more solitary and less common then the other it has no song it sits on the top twigs of odd trees or bushes in spring quivering its wings and uttering a pleasant 'cree creeing' note

The furze lark† is a led and brown colord bird with an odd white colord streak on each side the head down to the bill its nest is a curious one built of dead grass and lind with the fur of rabbits the brown linnet builds in furze and makes a similar‡ nest but in other respects the birds are quite distinct tho often confounded together by bird fanciers the male brown linnet has a beautiful red breast and the male furze larks a pale blue or lead colord one the furze larks eggs are very long and nearly white

The wood lark** [tree pipit] is of a dark brown not much unlike the hedge sparrow it sings as it decends from the trees flying in a slanting direction to the ground and rises and falls in alternate scotches as it decends which prolongs its song it builds its nest in a hazel or maple root and lays six eggs generaly very thickly spotted with dark spots

A bird which the common people call a clodhopper [wheatear] appears be of the lark tribe it is a brown slender bird and hops from clod to clod wagging its tail at the same time like a wagtail [A46, 114]

SKY LARK

a bird that is as of much use in poetry as the Nightingale account of one kept tame by a publican at Tallington [A46, 168]

---

* Author of a book on birds.
† This is a very puzzling bird. No European song-bird appears to have this combination of characters, the white eye-stripes and the blue-grey breast.
‡ Clare has written 'smilar'.   ** Clare has written 'like'.

Right happy bird so full of mirth
Mounting and mounting still more high
To meet morns sun shine in the sky
Ere yet it smiles on earth

How often I delight to stand
Listening a minutes space away
Where summer spreads one green away
By wheat or barly land

To see thee with a sudden start
The green and placid herbage leave
And in void air a vision weave
For joys delighted heart

Shedding to heaven a vagrant mirth
When silence husheth other themes
And woods in their dark splendour dreams
Like heaviness on earth

My mind enjoys the happy sight
To watch thee to the clear blue sky
And when I downward turn my eye
Earth glows with lonely light

Then nearer comes thy happy sounds
And downward drops thy little wing
And now the vallys hear thee sing
And all the dewy grounds

Gleam into joy — now from the eye
Thourt dropping sudden as a stone
And now thourt in the wheat alone
And still the circle of the sky

And Abscent like a pleasant good
Though many come within the way
Thy little song to peeping day
Is still remembered on

For who can cross green fields of corn
And see the sky lark start to meet the day
And not feel more delighted on his way
Upon a summers morn

Tis one of those heart cheering sights
On green earths rural chronicles
That upon every memory dwells
Among home fed delights

[A57, 78]

SKYLARK

GRASS HOPPER LARK [GRASSHOPPER WARBLER]
think this is our Cricket bird   [A46, 168]

Heard the Cricket Bird or Grasshopper Bunting last night (April 22)
[1825] making its odd chittering note   it exactly resembles the noise
that children make with their screekers as they are calld – and it
continues it for a minute together before it stops and then starts
agen   it began just as a shower begun and continued chittering on at

its odd song till night fall – I have seldom heard this bird any were but
in woods   [A46, 162]

> The cricket larks small inward whispering song
> Frets nights dull drowsy listings from sleep
>   [N17, 127]

WOOD LARK [TREE PIPIT]

builds its nest in the woods on the ground under a stoven with long
dead grass and lines it with horse hair and roots   lays 6 eggs of a
dirty white thickly swarmed all over with dusky spots   it has an odd
way of singing as it flyes from tree to tree dropping down a little way
and then rising up with a jerk and when the fly up they are silent
singing ever time the drop trembling their wings till they jerk up agen
and when they are weary they either stuntly drop on the ground or
settle on a tree where their song ceases till they are agen on the wing
                                                              [A46, 168]

> . . . Round each mossed stulp the woodlark hides her nest
> And delicate blue bell that her home surrounds
> Bows its soft fragrance oer her spotted breast
> Till from the boys rude steps she startled flyes
> Who turns the weeds away and vainly seeks the prize
>   [A41, 41]

*   *   *

> The woodlark rises from the coppice tree
> Time after time untired she upwards springs
> Silent while up then coming down she sings
> A pleasant song of varied melody
> Repeated often till some sudden check
> The sweet tuned impulse of her rapture stops
> Then stays her trembling wings and down she drops
> Like to a stone amid the crowding becks
> Where underneath some hazels mossy root
> Is hid her little low and humble nest
> Upon the ground larks love such places best
> And hers doth well her quiet station suit
> As safe as secresy her six eggs lie
> Mottled with dusky spots unseen by passers bye

Yet chance will somtimes prove a faithless guest
Leading some wanderer by her hants to roam
And startled by the rustle from her nest
She flutters out and so betrays her home
Yet this is seldom accident can meet
With her weed hidden and surrounded nest
Ive often wondered when agen my feet
She fluttered up and fanned the anemonie
That blossomed round in crowds – how birds could be
So wise to find such hidden homes again
And this in sooth has often puzzled me – they go
Far off and then return – but natures plain
She giveth what sufficeth them to know
That they of comfort may their share retain

Sweet little minstrel of the sunny summer
Housed in the pleasant swells that front the sun
Neighbour to many a happy yearly comer
For joys glad tidings when the winters done
How doth they music through the silk grass run
That cloaths the pleasant banks with herbage new

[A57, 36]

*   *   *

Among the lilys of the valleys there
The Woodlark hides its nest from robbing boys

[N17, 87]

Wagtail Tribe

GREY WAGTAIL [PIED WAGTAIL]

a common bird haunts brooks and water pudges builds its nest in old
walls and more commonly in the heaps of loose stones left in stone
pits makes a nest of longshaws and lines it with whool and horshair
somtimes builds in wood stacks lays 5 and six eggs of a white color
thickly spotted with black spots like the house sparrows account of a
young Cuckoo being found in a wagtails nest told me by Gordon   it
has no song but utters a short chirping while on the wing   it is seen
with us all the winter   [A46, 168]

The wagtail builds in woodstacks and in walls
Maids often find them when the faggot falls

[A9, 60]

GREAT GREY WAGTAIL [GREY WAGTAIL]

not common here   [A46, 168]

Saw this day a Female Yellow Wagta[il] January 16th 1830

[A45, loose double quarto inside covers]

YELLOW WAGTAIL

a beautiful bird leaves us in the winter and returns in april builds on
the ground among the grain makes its nest of straws dead grass and
twitch and lines it with hair somthing like a larks but deeper   the
eggs are spotted like the grey wagtails but darker   [A46, 168]

Warblers

NIGHTINGALE

[*Natural History Letter III*] I forgot to say in my last that the
Nightingale sung as common by day as night and as often tho its a
fact that is not generaly known   your Londoners are very fond of
talking about this bird and I believe fancy every bird they hear after
sunset a Nightingale   I remember when I was there last while
walking with a friend in the fields of Shacklwell we saw a gentleman
and lady listning very attentive by the side of a shrubbery and when
we came up we heard them lavishing praises on the beautiful song of
the nightingale which happend to be a thrush but it did for them and
they listend and repeated their praise with heart felt satisfaction
while the bird seemed to know the grand distinction that its song had
gaind for it and strove* exultingly to keep up the deception by
attempting a varied and more louder song   the dews was ready to
fall but the lady was heedless of the wet grass tho the setting sun as a
traveller glad to rest was leaning his enlargd rim on the earth like a
table of fire and lessening by degrees out of sight leaving night and a
few gilt clouds behind him   such is the ignorance of nature in large
Citys that are nothing less then over grown prisons that shut out the
world and all its beautys

* Clare has 'strive'.

NIGHTINGALE

The nightingale as I said before is a shoy bird   if any one approaches too near her secret haunts its song ceases till they pass when it is resumd as loud as before but I must repeat your quotation from Chaucer to illustrate this

> The new abashed nightingale
> That stinteth first when she beginneth sing
> When that she heareth any herde's tale
> Or in the hedges any wight stearing*
> And after siker doth her voice out ring

As soon as they have young their song ceases and is heard no more till the returning may   after they cease singing they make a sort of gurring guttural noise as if calling the young to their food I know not what its for else but they make this noise continually and doubtless before the young leave the nest   I have said all I can say about the Nightingale – In a thicket of black thorns near our village calld 'bushy close' we have great numbers of them every year but not so many as we usd to have   like the Martins and Swallows and other birds of passage they seem to diminish but for what cause I know not . . .   [A49, 43]

[*Same letter*] P.S. I can scarcly believe the account which you mention at the end of your letter respecting the mans 'puzzling himself with doubts about the Nightingales singing by day and about the expression of his notes wether they are grave or gay' – you may well exclaim 'what solemn trifling'   it betrays such ignorance that I can scarcely believe it – if the man does but go into any village solitude a few miles from London next may their varied music will soon put away his doubts of its singing by day – nay he may get rid of them now by asking any country clown the question for its such a common fact that all know of it – and as to the 'expression of its notes' if he has any knowledge of nature let him ask himself wether nature is in the habit of making such happy seeming songs for sorrow as that of the Nightingales – the poets indulgd in fancys but they did not wish that those matter of fact men the Naturalists shoud take them for facts upon their credit – What absurditys for a world that is said to get wiser and wiser every day . . .   [A49, R46]

I never had greater oppertunitys of observing the Nightigale then I

* wight stirring.

44

had this summer – because she was constantly as it were at my very door – she whistled without effort – never raising the feathers of her throat and neck and head as I had seen her but piping as quietly as the Robin and as if the song almost came involuntary without her knowing it – I watched her frequently and never saw her in that extacy as she seemed to be in when I have watched her in my old woods at Helpstone – as regards particulars this is in the wrong gender for I think and am *almost* certain that the female is silent and never sings [A58, 15]

I can sit at my window here and hear the nightingale singing in the orchard and I attempted to take down her notes but they are so varied that every time she starts again after the pauses seems to be somthing different to what she uttered before and many of her notes are sounds that cannot be written the alphabet having no letters that can syllable the sounds [A58, 10]

> The nightingale keeps tweeting churring round
> But leaves in silence when the nest is found
>
> [A61, 8]

May 29 [1830] My Frederick* found today saturday a Nightingales nest in the bottom of the orchard hedge with 4 eggs in it and tho there is but one oak tree as I am told in the Lordship she had got some oak leaves about her nest – in the woods she generally nay always uses dead oak leaves very plentifully at the bottom or outside of her nest and seldom or rarely puts any within side but here she had got dead grass on the outside and a few old oak leaves eaten bare to the fibres by insects withinside her nest and I never in my life as yet saw a nightingales nest without oak leaves and I have found a many and as many as seven one May in Bushy Close and Royce Wood at Help-stone [A58, 10]

The nightigales nest in the orchard hedge was composed without side of dead maple leaves and some oak leaves and lined within with withered grass and a few fragments of oak leaves [B8, 19]

June 8th – Seeing a Magpie today near the Nightingales nest I suspected it was stealing the young [and going] to see he found an

* Frederick Clare (1824–43), John Clare's eldest son.

45

empty nest – the old bird is singing this evening as usual tho in a seeming sadder way – yet we hope the young has escaped from the nest [A58, 9]

When the young of the Nightingale leave the nest the old ones bring them out of the woods into old hedgrows and bushy borders about the fields – where they seem to be continualy hunting along the roots and hedge bottoms for food   their hants here are easily known from the plaintive noise of 'toot toot' that the old ones are constantly making at passers bye where the path runing by a hedge side make such intrusions frequent – the fire tail and the Robin make a similar noise – the Nightingale often makes another noise of 'chur chur' which on hearing I have seen the young one instantly hopping down from the hedge into the bottom of the dyke and when she made the noise of 'toot toot' they would in a moment be all as still as if nothing was there but the old one   I always took the 'chur chur' as a food call and the tooting noise as a token of alarm [A49, 84]

I have often observed that many birds that are reckoned birds of passage are very bad flyers particularly the Nightingale which appears as timid on the wing as a young bird for fright it as you will it cannot be urged to venture earnest flight above the underwood but hops from twig to twig in short fluttering attempts as almost makes one doubt wether its a bird of any passage at all [A46, 139]

Birdcatchers say that the* maggot or grub that is bred in flower and is often found in the bings or other parts of great mills is a bait that never fails to catch them in the bird traps [A46, 162]

RED ROBIN/REDBREAST [ROBIN]

> The sparrow seeks his feathers for a nest
> And the fond robin with his ruddy breast
> Hops round the garden wall were thickly twine
> The leafing sweet briar and the propt woodbine
> And in a hole behind the thickening boughs
> He builds with hopeful joy his little house
> Stealing with jealous speed the wool and hair
> Were cows and sheep have lain them down to lair

* Clare repeats 'the'.

ROBIN

And pecks the green moss in his murmering glee
From cottage thatch and squatting apple tree
Tutling his song – [A21, 14]

RED START OR FIRE TAIL

comes latter end of April the male is a beautiful bird – builds in old
walls and hollows trees makes a nest of green moss lines it with wool
and cow hair lays 9 eggs and often more of a pale blue like the hedge
sparrows but smaller – makes a plaintive chirp [? in summer time]

[A46, 168]

The fire tail tells the boys when nests are nigh
And tweets and flyes from every passer bye
[A61, 8]

HEDGE SPARROW

. . . fond of building in gardens and homesteads it builds its nest in
hedges and in bushes near the bottom [A46, 169; *see also p. 32*, SPARROWS]

[*Natural History Letter* V] The Hedge sparrow may be called one of
these domestic birds for it is fond of frequenting gardens and home-
steads near villages it is a harmless peacable bird and not easily
alarmed at the approach of man its song is low and trifling it
builds its nest* early in the Spring in hedges and close bushes about
gardens and homsteads of green moss lined with† fine whool and
cow hair it lays 5 eggs of a very fine blue nay it may be calld a green
blue they are clear without spots it feeds on insects and small
seeds and is frequently robd of its eggs by the cuckoo who leaves one
of her own in its stead which the hedge sparrow hatches and brings
up with an unconsous fondness and if she lays any more eggs of her
own after the cuckoo has deposited hers it is said that the young
cuckoo has the instinct to thrust the young sparrows out of the nest
to occupy it himself wether this be true or not I cannot say for
I have never witnessd it tho I have fond a young cuckoo in the
hedge sparrows nest and in the Wagtails also but in no other birds
beside these too seem to be the selected foster parents of its
young The hedge sparrow is very early at building its nest I found
one last year in a box tree with three eggs on the 3rd of Febuary the
birds had built in the same bush 3 years together – a sharp blast

* Clare repeats the word 'nest'. † Clare repeats 'with'.

happend when the young was just hatchd and perishd them and the
brought off another brood in the same nest [A49, 61]

SEDGE BIRD [SEDGE WARBLER]

this bird is a good deal like the white throat but larger   it build its
nest a mong the sedge in marshey places of dead bents and airiff
clung together with little knotts of spiders webbs often seen hanging
among flowers lined with hair   it is a deep thin nest and may be seen
thro like a thin plaited basket   its eggs are like the white throats of a
dull white speckeld with bluish and brown spots   it dwells in
meadows and low places has a variety of short notes that can hardly
be calld a song [A46, 169]

WHITE THROAT

a bird little known celebrated for its song which often imitates the
nightingale in* variety and loudness build in woods on black thorns
generaly a thin carless nest of bents lined with hairs   lays 5 eggs of a
dirty greens white spotted with brown and joceolat spots
  Small whitethroat builds a nest of materials like the former but
it chuses low clumps of brambles near the ground and I have often
found it in beds of the keen nettle curiously fixd between them   its
eggs are white with small dirty spots   it is as small as the wren and
when frit from its nest it hops out and runs on the ground in a
serpentine direction so as to be readily mistake for a mouse [A46, 169]

> The happy white throat on the sweeing bough
> Swayed by the impulse of the gadding wind
> That ushers in the showers of april – now
> Singeth right joyously and now reclined
> Croucheth and clingeth to her moving seat
> To keep her hold and till the wind for rest
> Pauses she mutters inward melody
> That seems her hearts rich thinkings to repeat
> And when the branch is still her little breast
> Swells out in raptures gushing symphonies
> And then against her brown wing softly prest
> The wind comes playing an enraptured guest
> This way and that she swees – till gusts arise
> More boisterous in their play – when off she flies

* Clare has 'and'. [B8, R113]

WILLOW BITER [WILLOW WARBLER]

it is of yellow greenish color haunts willow trees and may be seen
[? busily] runing up the willow branches pecking at the young twigs
whence its name   it builds in the crevices and holes of decayed
willows   I never found its nest with eggs tho I have found them with
young   [A46, 169]

   you are very right as to the Willow Wrens building in holes of
trees if that is what you alude to   I only know of two sorts of the
Willow Wrens one larger then the other and of a lighter green   the
small one I believe comes first   they are called among the common
people here 'Willow biters'* from their pecking the young twigs
of willow on their first coming for inscects that lye between the
bark   both of the[m] builds in the holes of trees and lays white eggs
spotted with feint red spots – as for naturalists you must not let them
go before your own observations for some of them are 'naturals'
indeed – they often pass their own fancys off for facts and on this I
shoud suppose is the reason that so many foolish lyes have been
uttered respecting the nightingale   [A46, 156]

> The willow biter builds agen the dyke
> A small round nest and all lay eggs alike
>   [B9, 60]

LITTLE WILLOW WREN [CHIFFCHAFF]

I think this is the little green bird that haunts woods and solitary
places and builds its nests on the [? roots] or on a small twig near it of
green moss lined with feathers   it is often mistaken for the Wrens
                                                           [A46, 169–70]

PETTICHAP [CHIFFCHAFF]

a little bird about the size of the wren that has a note somthing like
'Pettichap' whence its name   this note it keeps repeating as it hops
about the tops of trees   I never yet coud see one to examine it as
they are constantly in motion and genneraly buried† in the closest
thickets   it makes a curious nest in low bushes   I saw one to day in
Gunworth Ferry Thicket at Milton   [A46, 169]

---

* Clare does not close the inverted commas after opening them before 'Willow'.
† Clare has 'bured'.

[1829] Have found this year upon minute observation that the Pettichap makes what may be considered a wide entrance in her oven nest for her size but the largest I found would not admit 3 fingers without stretching the nest and perhaps they may both sit on the eggs together at night as it were impossible for one bird to cover them all – I have also noticed that all the oven building birds such as titmice willow biters pettichaps &c lay a great number of eggs 9 to 10

[A49, 86]

GOLDCREST

GOLDEN CRESTED WREN [GOLDCREST]

so calld from having a narrow line of a bright yellow rising on its crown   it is less then the wren   it builds a very curious nest on the pine trees in Milton Park hanging it from the branches and hanging it together with the glutinous substance or raisin that oozes from the grains and were this is not to be had it fastens its moss and other substances to gether like a basket   I have never got a nest with eggs   it is very common about the shrubberys in Milton near the Hall but I hear from Artis that they are the smallest eggs among birds

[A46, 170]

The Golden crested Wren makes a small nest resembling in shape the red caps and Pinks – but instead of placing it on the branch as they do – it hangs it underneath the branch and always build on the firdale – laying 7 or 8 eggs of a dull colour spotted with brown   [A46, 152]

WREN OR JINNEY WREN

. . . it somtimes builds by the sides of trees but not often   [A46, 170]

[*Natural History Letter VII*]* . . . The Wren is another of these domestic birds that has found favour in the affections of man   the hardiest gunner will rarely attempt to shoot either of them and tho it loves to haunt the same places as the Robin it is not so tame and never ventures to seek the protection of man in the hardest winter blasts   it finds its food in stackyards and builds its nest mostly in the roof of hovels and under the eaves of sheds about the habitations of man tho it is often found in the cowsheds in closes and sometimes aside the roots of underwood in the woods   its nest is made of green moss and lined with feathers   the entrance is a little hole in the side like a corkhole in a barrel   it lays as many as 15 or 16 white eggs very small and faintly spotted with pink spots   it is a pert bird among its fellows and always seems in a conscieted sort of happiness with its tail strunted up oer its back and its wings dripping down – its song is more loud then the Robins and very pleasant tho it is utterd in broken raptures by sudden starts and as sudden endings   it begins to sing in march and continues till the end of spring when it becomes moping and silent . . .   [A49, 60]

REED WREN [REED WARBLER]

the nest of this bird is a very curious one and the insides is as round and not much larger then the inside of an hens eggshell   it builds the out side of dead blades of grass small water weeds and lines it in a very workman like manner with the down of the old last year reeds   I found one near the horse pit in the meadow   they build by the water side in low bushes and sometimes among the reed   it is like the sedge wobbler but smaller   its eggs are of a dirty color markd with irregular lines or longs dots at the large end and paler ones and smaller intermixd   [A46, 170]

* This comes after a passage on the robin, for which see *Selected Poems and Prose of John Clare*, pp. 90–1.

A little slender bird of reddish brown
With frequent haste pops in and out the reeds
And on the river frequent flutters down
As if for food and so securely feeds
Her little young that in their ambush needs
Her frequent journeys hid in thickest shade
Where danger never finds a path to throw
A fear on comforts nest securely made
In woods of reeds round which the waters flow
Save by a jelted stone that boys will throw
Or passing rustle of the fishers boat
It is the reed bird prized for pleasant note
Ah happy songster man can seldom share
A spot so grudgd [and] hidden from the hants of care
[A57, 33]

WHEAT EAR

builds on Caistor Old Field and on Emmonsails   their nests is
somtimes found by the cow boys   they build on the ground and
often in the old neglected rabbit holes   I have never seen their nests
[A46, 170; see p. 37, LARKS]

WIN CHAT [WHINCHAT]

I think I have seen this bird often in the Milton stone Quarries on the
heath and I believe it* is often calld a flye catcher or a spider catcher –
I never found its nest that I know of   [A46, 170]

STONE CHAT

I think this bird is what the common people with us call the Short
taild Wagtail – it frequents Milton stone quarrys on the heath and is
a good deal like the smaller grey wagtail   it builds in loose heaps of
stones and in the crevices of the loose rocks   it does not flye in ups
and downs like the wag tail but flutters with short flights about the
quarries   it is found on different parts of the heath seemlingly fond
of lone places   [A46, 170]

Chats – people in villages have a many names for one bird which they
confound/distinguish as many birds – they talk of Hay chats straw
chats nettle chats &c – Its eggs are blotched with lead and dirty green

* Clare has 'is'.

STONECHAT

The stone chat is a very handsome bird   it visits southorp heath
and builds about the stone pits   [A46, 146]

Flycatcher Tribe

PIED FLY CATCHER [SPOTTED FLYCATCHER]

not very common here builds in walls and under the eaves of stacks
and ricks like the sparrow   they dont spare for stuff making a very
large nest   [A46, 170]

Titmouse Tribe

BLACK CAP [GREAT TIT]

a common bird of which there are two varietys the large and
small   the small [marsh tit] is frequent in woods hopping about the
grains of the oaks and making a twitting noise   they are often in
companys of 10 or a dozen together   I think they build in old wood
peckers holes but I have not found their nest   the large black cap
builds in old walls makes a nest like the blue cap of moss and cowhair
and lays from five to nine egg larger then the blue caps of a clear
white freckled with pink spots   [A46, 169]

The Blackcap
Under the twigs the black cap hangs in vain
With snow white patch streaked over either eye
This way and that he turns and peeps again
As wont where silk-cased insects used to lie
But summer leaves are gone the day is bye
For happy holidays and now he fares
But cloudy like the weather yet to view
He flirsts a happy wing and inly wears
Content in gleaning what the orchard spares
And like his little couzin capped in blue
Domesticates the lonely winter through
In homestead plots and gardens where he wears
Familiar pertness – yet but seldom comes
With the tame robin to the door for crumbs
                                          [A54, 433]

*   *   *

The black cap builds in trees where boys can see
The eggs and scarce get finger in the tree

[B9, 60]

BLUE TITMOUSE [BLUE TIT]

it is reckoned destructive to the young buds of trees by gardiners who take every means to destroy it   it. may be seen at spring busily employd hopping from twig to twig about the apple trees   it is very fond of hanging by its legs under the branches and looking upwards into buds &c this is a [   ] pecuuliar to titmice and they may be often seen in this situation   [A46, 170]

The blue cap hid in lime kilns out of sight
Lays nine small eggs and spoted red and white
And oft in walls where boys a noisey pest
Will pull a stone away to get the nest

[B9, 60]

LONG TAILD TITMOUSE [LONG-TAILED TIT]

or Bumbarrel Pudding bags Feather pokes . . .   [A46, 171]

[*Natural History Letter V*] . . . The long taild Titmouse calld with us Bumbarrel and in yorkshire pudding bags and feather pokes is an early builder of its nest   it makes a very beautiful one in the shape of an egg leaving an entrance on one side like the wren   it forms the outside of grey moss and lines it with great quantitys of feathers   it lays a great number of very small eggs   I have found them with 18 they are very small of a white color sprinkled with pink spots at the larger end   one might think that by the number of eggs these birds lay they woud multiply very vast but on the contrary they are not half so plentiful as other birds for the small hawks make a terrible havock among their young broods as soon as they leave their nests – its song is low and pretty the young ones that escape the school boy and hawk live in familys and never forsake their parents till the next spring – they may be seen to the number of 20 in winter picking somthing off the twigs of the white thorn in the hedgerows   [A49, 53]

The oddling bush close shelterd – hedge new plashd
Of which springs early likeing makes a guest
First with a shade of green though winter dashed
There full as soon bumbarrels make a nest

LONG-TAILED TIT

Of mosses grey with cobwebs closely tyed
And warm and rich as feather bed within
With little hole on its contrary side
That pathway peepers may no knowledge win
Of what her little oval nest contains
Ten eggs and often twelve with dusts of red
Soft frittered – and full soon the little lanes
[   ] the young crowd and hear the twittering song
Of the old birds who call them to be fed
While down the hedge they hop and hide along

[A57, 15]

MARSH TIT MOUSE OR BLACK CAP [MARSH TIT]

This is what we call the little black cap   it hants woods and Ozier
holts and builds in the neglected holes of the small Wood pecker   it
keeps con[s]tantly in motion hopping among the oak tops and
pecking uttering a double tootling note at the same time   [A46, 171]

[MARSH OR WILLOW TIT]

[*Natural History Letter IX*] [25 March 1825] . . . the Ivy berrys too
are quite ripe and the wood pigeons are busily fluskering among the
Ivied dotterels on the skirts of the common   they are very fond of
them – and a little namless bird with a black head and olive green
back and wings – not known – it seems to peck the Ivy berries for its
food and I have remarked that it comes as soon as they are ripe to the
Ivy trees and dissapears from them when they are gone – I fancy it is
of the tribe of the Tit mice and I have often found a nest clinging by
the side of trees among the Ivy which I think belongs to it   I know
nothing further of its Life and habits – I think I had the good luck
today to hear the bird which you spoke of last March as singing early
in spring and which you apropriatly named the mock nightingale
for some of its notes are exactly similar   I heard it singing in 'Open
Wood' and was startled at first to think it was the nightingale and
tryd to creep in to the thicket to see if I coud discover what bird it was
but it seemd to be very shoy and got farther from me as I approachd
till I gave up the pursuit – I askd some Woodmen who were planting
under wood at the time wether they knew the bird and its song seemd
to be very familiar to them   they said it always came with the first
fine days of spring and assured me it was the wood chat but they
coud not agree with each others opinion for another believd it to be

the large black cap or black headed Titmouse so I coud get nothing
for fact but I shall keep a sharp look out when I hear it again —. . .

[A49, 67]

[WILLOW TIT]

The March Nightingale

Now sallow catkins once all downy white
Turn like the sunshine into golden light
The rocking clown leans oer the spinney rail
In admiration at the sunny sight
The while the Blackcap doth his ears assail
With such a rich and such an early song
He stops his own and thinks the nightingale
Hath of her monthly reckoning counted wrong
'Sweet jug jug jug' comes loud upon his ear
Those sounds that unto may by right belong
Yet on the awthorn scarce a leaf appears
How can it be – spell struck the wondering boy
Listens again – again the sound he hears
And mocks it in his song for very joy

[A40, 30]

Swallow Tribe

CHIMNEY SWALLOW [SWALLOW]

they come about the middle of april and I observe on their first visit
that they follow the course of brooks and rivers   I have observed
this for years and always found them invariably pursuing their first
flights up the brinks of the meadow streams and I have always
observed that they come eastward   they build their nests in chim-
neys of dust straw and feathers generaly chusing the side were the
currents of smoke is the strongest   they lay 5 eggs of a dirty white
freckled with pink spots   they often make their nest under brig
arches in barns and out houses under the rig trees entering thrg a hole
in the walls or door way and when I was a boy I found one yearly
under a low arch that overstrid a dyke at the entrance to wood croft
house – they collect together in the autumn and learn their young to
flye who at first take short circuits and then flye on their chimneys to
rest when the old ones come and feed them   when more used to flye
they venture wider circuits and leave the place were they was bred

59

altogether chusing the bartlements of the church as a place of rest –
they gennerally haunt rivers and brooks before they start and may be
seen settling 4 or 5 together on twigs of Osiers beside the stream that
bend with them till they nearly touch the water – they make west-
ward when they start and often return agen resting by flocks on
churches and trees in the village as if they were making attempts
before they started for good   [A46, 171]

Swallows (but wether the chimney swallows I know not) build on the
beam of a shed in Milton gardens which support the roof by running
from end to end of the building – they have a very odd appearance
and are placed in the same manner as a saucer on a mantel piece or a
bason on a shelf and look exactly as if put there   [A49, 83]

SWALLOW

[? 1811] July 21st   To day a young Swallow scarcely pen feathered
fell down the chimney where it lay chirping a good while – at last the
parent birds ventured down and fed it – and a short time after 2 other
swallows joined them and by some means or other got the young one
up to its nest in the chimney top   [A48, 43]

Emigrating swallows now
Sweep no more the green hills brow
Nor in circuits round the spring
Skim and dip their sutty wing
And no more their chimney high
Twitter round to catch the flye
But with more majestic rise
Practicing their exersise
And their young broods to pursue
Autumns weary journney through
Meditating travels long
Try boldest flights without a song
To leave our winters cold sojourn
And come no more till springs return

[A50, 78]

MARTIN [HOUSE MARTIN]

Martins do not come till after the swallow and seldom make their appearance till may   they make their nests under the eaves of houses were some people deem them sacred and reckon the appearance of a Martins Nest under their eaves as a good Omen and as a charm against thunder and lighting for which also the large house leek is considerd an infallable safe guard and planted on the rigs of roofs for that purpose – Childern are cautioned not to destroy them in the fear of incurring therebye almost an unforgiven offence to their maker and if a hardend boy happens to destroy one his parents consider that somthing serious will befall him   thus they gain an asylum under most cottages by this tender and praise worthy superstition were otherwise they woud find none   they* line their nests with straw and feathers and lay 5 eggs nearly white but on close examination they are shadowd with feint red spots – the Sparrow is an unfeeling enemey to these birds and when its nest is nearly finished they will take it by storm and make use of it them selves   in these emergencies the martins will both occupy the nest and keep in for days together while the besieging robbers sit as patiently on the thatch above watching the opertunity to enter and when the Martins are pined out and forced to leave their nest for food the cock sparrow seizes the chance imediatly and the poor martins find on their return a determined occupant who resists their every effort to regain the

* Clare has 'their'.

lawful possesion of their houses – some times they return the insult afterwards by an odd revenge when the old sparrows leave the nest for food as they will do when they have been in quiet possesion of it awhile   they instantly sally to the nest were others of their companions as I have often seen join help in hand and block up the entrance till the hole is too small for the sparrows to enter who on their return may fancy some stragedee is laid to entrap them leave it with little or no hessitation to regain an entrance – for I have observed that the sparrow cannot get into the hole of a finished nest who always watches the oppertunity to seize the possesion before she has finished the entrance adding the lining of straw and feathers themselves and one of these may easily be known by straw hanging out of the hole as they use more lining then the martin   [A46, 172]

SAND MARTIN

We have none of these in our neeghbourhood but they are very numerous about the upland neighbourhood and a man with whom I burnt lyme said they build their nests by scrores on the side of a quarry were he worked near Northampton   [A46, 171]

Sand martins make holes in the side of a sand or stone pit going strat* for a good way and then turning stunt where they are widened and there a loose nest is formed of dead grass small leaves and twitch – I have also noticed that all the nests in the same side of a stone pit have the turning at the end made the same way – and if the stone pit points from north to south they are all turned to the left hand or southward   [A46, 189]

SWIFT

this comes last and retires the earliest   it remains the longest on the wing and continues its circuit round churches and old castles   it makes a curious nest of cobwebs lined with hair or feathers lays 5 eggs freckled with dark spots it builds in crevices of the church walls and in large houses were boys find very difficult access to get it   the parish clerk found an old one in the church last year that lay on the ground with its wings spread out in an helpless posture as if dead he broght it to me and set it were I woud   it coud not flye nor ever made the least attempt its legs was very short and muffled with feathers like a bantum its wings very long and narrow and I observed

* Clare presumably meant to write 'strait', i.e. straight.

SAND MARTIN

at the fore corner of each eye a small tuft of feathers which nearly hid
them   this I suppose was a convenience of nature to keep the sharp
air from hurting the eyes as the swiftness of their flight must have
made the wind very sharp   [A46, 171–2]

>   The develing black as coal comes out at night
>   And flyes above the village out of sight
>   They build in holes and straws and feathers fetch
>   And build above the tallest ladders reach
>   They make a nest like sparrows and more high
>   And build where sparrows seldom care to flye
>   They fly above the swallows far away
>   And never seem to settle all the day
>   They build where few men seldom get for fear
>   And keep the self same hole from year to year
>   Yet boys will dare when danger cannot rest
>   And walk upon the slates and get the nest
>   Ive never seen the eggs but hear them say
>   Theyre spotted like the sparrows white and grey
>   [B9, 77]

NIGHT JAR

not common here but found on Emmonsales heath   the make a
carless nest of loose grass on the ground and lay 3 eggs not unlike the
Wood owls of a yellowish white blotchd largly with dark spots
                                                   [A46, 172]

[*Natural History Letter II*] The Fern Owl or Goat sucker or Night jar
or night hawk while sevearl more or's might be added no doubt to
fresh names is a curious bird   they are found about us in summer on
a wild heath calld Emmingsales and I believe that is the only spot
which they visit   they make an odd noise in the evening begining at
dewfall and continuing it at intervals all night   it is a beautifull
object in Poetic Nature – (nay all nature is poetic)   from that
peculiarity alone one cannot pass over a wild heath in a summer
evening without being stopt to listen and admire its novel and
pleasing noise   it is a trembling sort of crooing sound which may
be nearly imitated by making a crooing noise and at the same
time patting the finger before the mouth to break the sound like
stopping a hole in the German flute to quaver a double sound on one

NIGHTJAR

note   this noise is generally made as it descends from a bush or tree
for its prey   it is said to feed on insects that breed on the fox fern
whense its name   it is a beautiful mottld bird variously shadowd
with the colors of black and brown   it appears of the hawk tribe*
its eye is keen its bill hookshapd and its mouth very wide with long
bristle like hairs growing at each corner   my friend Artis has one in
his collection of specimens and knows a great deal more about its
habits then I do   there was a nest of one of these birds found on
Emmingsales last year by the Cow keepers with 3 eggs in it wether
the whole number I cannot say   they was describd to me as short
and smallish eggs blotchd with umber colord spots   I believe the
nest was found among the brakes   it was sent to Dr Skrimshire of
Peterbro who is a curious man and collects the eggs of English
birds   I never found a nest of these birds in my life so I cannot say
were they build but the next time I visit Artis or Henderson† I will
enquire and send you further particulars   as beautiful an object as
this bird must have been in the summer dewfall rambles of Poets I
have never read one that mentions it except Mrs Smith in her
Sonnets‡ which I had the pleasure to meet with last summer in a
friends book case   her poems may be only pretty but I felt much
pleasd with them because she wrote more from what she had seen of
nature then from what she had read of it   therefore those that read
her poems find new images which they had not read of before tho
they have often felt them and from those assosiations poetry derives
the power of pleasing in the happiest manner   When I workd at
Casterton I met with another nocturnal bird calld a 'night hawk'   I
say another because I am certain it was not the Fern owl it was
larger   I have started it in the night from among the short stumpy
bushes on the cow pasture often but coud not distinguish the color or
make of the bird   all I coud tell of it was that it seemd very swift on
the wing and from that I imagind it of the hawk kind – My Love
rambles then made me acquainted with many of the privacys of night
which she seemd wishing to keep as secrets   I was then the compan-
ion of the Evening and very often the morning Star   Pattys Lodge
stood in a lone spot and the very path seemd to loose itself in the
solitudes and was glad to take the direction of rabbit tracks ere it
coud lead one to the door   nature revelld in security   this bird was

* Clare has 'trible'.
† See footnotes pp. 4 and 6.
‡ Charlotte Smith, *Elegiac Sonnets* (London, 1784).

one of her curositys   it very often startld me with its odd noise
which was a dead thin whistling sort of sound which I fancied was
the whistle call of robbers for it was much like the sound of a man
whistling in fear of being heard by any but his companions tho it was
continued much longer then a man coud hold his breath   it had no
trembling in it like a gamekeeps dog-whistle but was of one thin
continued sound   I was supprisd when I mentiond it to them to find
it was the noise of a bird and of one very common about there   it
was not only heard in sumer but at all seasons of the year   they
knew no other name for it then that of the Night hawk and they
supposd it preyd on the young rabbits by night and made their
burrows its hiding place by day as it was never seen after the
mornings twilight began   it made no noise when it was startld up in
my hearing so I supposd from that it was mostly sitting when it made
its fear creeping and danger haunting cry – Querie – May it not be
very natural to suppose that the frequent whistles which people have
heard while crossing wild heaths under the horrible apprehesions of
being pursued by robbers came from this bird   I know not wether
Naturalists are acquainted with this curious circumstance neither
have I read sufficiently to know what opinions they give of it if they
are   I firmly believe it is a different spieces from the night jar of the
hawk tribe who like the owl is a nocturnal plunderer that hides in the
day from the light and glaring of the sun – if you have read of any
thing that resembles this bird I shall be glad to hear of it   I think the
noise cannot be unknown to curious observers in nature tho it lives
at a time when the Naturalist and Poet are not expected to be on their
rambles unless by accident which is very often the friend and cause to
new discoverys for the time when its call is the most often repeated is
at the dead of night between the hours of eleven and one before and
after this it is but seldom heard –. . .   [A49, 39]

Pigeon Tribe

STOCKDOVE

> Less timid now in many a flock
> The stock doves shun their solitude
> And crowd in fields with friendly stock
> To share the turnips winter food
>   [A48, 19]

RING DOVE [WOOD-PIGEON]

they are so common as not to need a description of their nests or eggs – my tame ones begin to want to couple and as there is no cock bird among them they often want to get their liberty to seek a mate – they will begin very orderly to build a nest of sticks if any be thrown in the cage and pull any thing into it for that purpose within reach – two of them has this season concieved a great hatred against the other and they have beat it so much that I was forced to take it out of the cage or they woud have killed it – they do not show that fondness for each other in their amourous moods as the coat piegon whom I have often observed at spring sitting on the coat and feeding each other and expressing many other symptms of fondness and affection [A46, 173]

WOOD PIEGONS

Our Lanscape is not poetical enough I shoud suspect for the far famd turtle dove tho I hear it breeds in Kent and Essex we have nothing more then the wood pigeon here which is a very poetical object in nature both from its soft cooing voice and its rustling rambles in the forrest foliage they are very shoy and nothing but a hard winter can make them bold when they leave the woods in large flocks and feed on the turnips with the sheep in spring they feed on the ivy berrys of which they seem very fond as one may often hear them rustling among the old ivy featherd dotterels and see them feeding in a greedy manner when the ploughmen begin seedtime they get plenty of grain* and then they begin there cooing song between that time and harvest it is a time of scarcity with them when they may be seen pecking up the young leaves of clover in a clover ground or gathering that green that covers ponds in summer calld duckmeat I believe they have no notion of feeding on the bents like the coat piegon when the harvest begins their cooing songs are resumd when they build their carless nest of sticks and breed – they never lay more then two eggs but they often breed twice or thrice in the year the young are coverd with a golden down and tho the old ones are shoy the young ones seem bold in their ignorance and when one approaches they even put themselves in a posture of defiance and make a puffing noise and they make a pecking motion at the hand that approaches to take them – I had 4 tame ones and have 3 left now one having got wounded while absent from home by a gun of which wounds it dyd

* Clare has 'grian'.

WOOD-PIGEON

the others are all hen birds and have layd this summer   it is said that they cannot be thouroghly tamd   perhaps they cannot but I believe that they might be tamd in the same way as the cote piegon for when ever mine get out they are sure to return in the evening   they have often been absent for 5 or 6 days and have at last sufferd themselves to be taken by the hand tho not by strangers   it woud not be a bad plan to try the experiment of domesticating this bird in a cote as they are very large – I put sticks in the cage and they make a nest of them each helping the other and one nest serves all but not as the first left for they each pull it to pieces and build it over again   they are very fond of each other and make a low cooing trembling their wings and picking each others feathers with their bills   I think if the cock bird had been alive they woud have bred tho the cage was much too small even for a pair for before I knew they was all hen birds I left the eggs in the cage and they broke them in flying down from the perch – they wanted to sit several days after they had laid and even now have not forgot it   these birds are beautiful objects in the summer landscape not only from the sweet murmur of their song but from their appearence on the wing   they make a startling rustle as they leave their nest or perch from a thick bush or tree   in breeding time they flye after each other in couples among the green trees and by clapping their wings in a sharp manner make a peculiar noise like the clapping of hands   they like to build in odd bushes about the fields were provision is in plenty or in ivy dotterels but it is mostly in hedgrows or on the margin of woods near the grain for they leave the barren solitudes and seem to prefer a dangerd plenty to security   [A46, 137]

Roaming the little path neath dotterel trees
Of some old hedge or spinney side Ive oft
Been startled pleasantly from musing ways
By frighted dove that suddenly aloft
Spiring through the many boughs with chittering noise
Till free from such restraints above the head
They smacked their clapping wings for very joys
And in a curious wood Ive oft been led
To climb the twig surrounded trunk and there
On some few bits of sticks two white eggs bye
As left by accident all lone and bare
Almost without a nest yet bye and bye
Two birds in golden down will leave the shells

And hiss and snap at wind blown leaves that shake
Around their home where green seclusion dwells
Till fledged and then the young adventurers take
The old ones timid flights from oak to oak
Listening the pleasant sutherings of the shade
Nor startled by the woodmans hollow stroke
Till autumns pleasant visions pine and fade
Then they in bolder crowds will sweep and flye
And brave the desert of a winter sky

[A57, 38]

GALLINACEOUS BIRDS

Pheasant Tribe

PHEASANT

makes its nest on the ground in bushy borders on the sides of
commons and sometimes in woods side tho seldom as the Fox is its
mortal enemey there and endued with ready sagasity to find the
nest   it lays 16, 18, and often 20 eggs of a plain green ash color like
the Partridge but larger   as soon as the birds are hatchd they leave
the nest and follow the hen Pheasant* who clucks and calls them like
a hen   in sitting time the old ones sit so close on the nest as to be
easily taken   a fellow last year found a nest in a wheat close by the
wood side   she sat hard and he caught her on the nest   the next day
he went agen and the Cock had taken her place and sat on the eggs
but he did not sit so close as the hen and flew off before the unfeeling
fellow caught him – I was told of the nest and went twice when the
Cock bird was on but the third time somthing had destroyd the eggs
and wether the Cock followd the fate of the hen I cannot tell   he
appeard to sit in good earnest as if he intended to hatch them   There
is sometimes a Variety of these birds found   I saw one last year
which I fancied a hen the color of the cock that wanted the red rim
round the eye and had a short tail and pure White ones are somtimes
found here generaly cocks   one Henderson got and stuffed the other
Pheasants* having fought and beaten it to death – they live on insects
in summer and on acorns and hips and Awes in Autumn and winter and
are very fond of a sort of little fungus that grows on the oak leaves
and drop off towards autum – the young ones if hatchd under a hen
are hard to tame or raise up yet it is sometimes done and I knew an old
woman fond of fowl that raised a Cock bird till it was as tame as the
fowl in the yard and it cohabited with the hens but its breed lost most
of likness of the Pheasant* and took more after the hens   [A46, 173–4]

It has been supposed by naturalists who are more fond of
starting new theories then proving old facts that our yard fowl the

* Clare has 'Peasant'.

Cock was origionaly from the wild pheasant but I think this is merely
a wide suposition as the yard cock always claps his wings and then
crows while the pheasant cock always crows first and claps his wings
afterwards   [A46, 155]

There was two milk white Pheasants shot here last year and one of
them was preservd by my friend Henderson   I know not wether
they are curositys or wether such things are common   [A46, 114]

Tetrao Genus

PARTRIDGE

scrats a hole in the wheat lands and makes no nest lays from 14 to 18
eggs of an ash color like the p[h]easants but less   the young ones run
as soon as they leave the shells – the partridge has a very pleasant call
in the evening among the wheat calling its mate or young together –
it is not a timid bird but on the shooting season is pursued with such
unfeeling anxiety by the sportsman and his dogs that it seems to
loose all fear in the confusion and will flye into a house or any were
from danger and suffer itself to be taken by the hand – one enterd a
house next door to mine last year and seemd as tame and as confident
of protection as a chicken but the tenant being as heartless as the
sportsmen it was killd and eaten – a very curious one with barred*
wings and a blue patch like the jay bird was shot in Allwalton field by
a gentleman and sent as a curosity to Mr Artis   [A46, 174]

> The partridge makes no nest but on the ground
> Lays many eggs and I have often found
> Sixteen or eighteen in a beaten seat
> When tracing oer the fields or weeding wheat
> They lay in furrows or an old land rig
> Brown as the pheasants only not so big
> Theyre often found by pasture boys at play
> And by the weeders often taen away
> The boys will often throw the eggs abroad
> And stay and play at blind eggs on the road
> They lay in any hole without a nest
> And oft a horses footing pleases best

* Clare has 'bared'.

And there they safely lie till weeders come
When boys half fill their hats and take them home

[B9, 99]

*　　*　　*

One day accross the fields I chancd to pass
When chickens chelped and skuttled in the grass
And as I looked about to find the seat
A wounded partridge dropped agen my feet
She fluttered round and calling as she lay
The chickens chelped and fluttered all away
I stooped to pick her up when up she drew
Her wounded wing and cackled as she flew
I wondered much to hear the chickens lye
As still as nothing till I wandered bye
And soon she came agen with much ado
And swept the grass and called them as she flew
But still they kept their seat and left no trace
And old cows snorted when they passed the place

[B9, 96]

QUAIL

The quail is in shape and color very much like the Partridge but
smaller   it is a very shy bird and is seldom urged to take wing   they
make a nest on the ground with long grass in the meadow grounds or
wheat field   they lay a great number of eggs like the partridge from
10 to 16 and 18   they are shorter and smaller then the partridge of a
greenish white spotted with lilac and dark joccolate spots   they
resemble the more hens in color as the landrail does those of the
Pewet – it is called wet myfoot by the common people from its note
which exactly resembles those words and when weeders and hay
makers hear it frequently repeat it they give out that it will be wet
which they consider a certain sign – I used to find several of their
nests when I was a boy by following the mowers and I never found
them with less then 9 and often with as many as 18   they differ from
the partridge P[h]easant and Landrail by putting grass in the hole for
a nest as the others never do – the young ones leave the nest as soon
as hatchd and run very swift – when the old one sits she sits very
close   I have heard my father say that he has mown over them
before the old one woud fly off   they are birds of passage and come
in may   I have heard them about the 10th never earlier   [A46, 175]

74

[*Natural History Letter VI*]* . . . The quail is almost as much of a mystery in the summer landscape and comes with the green corn like the quail† tho it is seen more often and is more easily urgd to take wing it makes an odd noise in the grass as if it said 'wet my foot wet my foot' which Weeders and Haymakers hearken to as a prophecy of rain and believe in it as an infallable sign   they are less then the Partridge and rise not unlike them when they take wing   they lay on the ground and seem to prefer the meadow grass to the cornfields as their nests are oftenest found in the meadows while the Landrakes

QUAIL

taste seems the contrary   the quail like the other lays a great quantity of eggs   I have found them with 16   they are smallish for the size of the bird and very near the color of the More hens but not half so large being about the size of the small thrushes‡   I understand they grow very bold while in the act of sitting   my father tells me while writing this that he has often mown over them in hay time

---

* This comes after a passage on the landrail, or corncrake, for which see *Selected Poems and Prose of John Clare*, p. 67.
† Clare must have intended 'landrail' here.
‡ Clare has 'thruses'.

when the bird woud not flye up but run about the swaths and squat down as if on her nest several times ere she took to wing – beautiful as these two images are in the book of nature [i.e. the corncrake and the quail] the poets have hardly mentiond them . . .   [A49, 56]

I wandered out one rainy day
And heard a bird with merry joys
Cry wet my foot for half the way
I stood and wondered at the noise

When from my foot a bird did flee
The rain flew bouncing from her breast
I wondered what the bird could be
And almost trampled on her nest

The nest was full of eggs and round
I met a shepherd in the vales
And stood to tell him what I found
He knew and said it was a quails

For he himself the nest had found
Among the wheat and on the green
When going on his daily round
With eggs as many as fifteen

Among the stranger birds they feed
Their summer flight is short and slow
Theres very few know where they breed
And scarcely any where they go
                      [A61, 78]

Crane Tribe

WHITE SPOON BILL [SPOONBILL]
one shot here about 12 years back   [A46, 175]

HERON
they feed on frogs toads and snakes as well as fish   they build on tall trees in rookerys like crows of twenty or thirty together   they make a nest of sticks and line it with wool leaving a hole in the bottom for

the young ones to put their legs thro as they are way long   they lay
from 3 to 5 eggs not as large as a hens of a slender shape and a dirty
yellowish ash color spoted and scrawled with brown and reddish
lines and spots – they are said never to meddle with the fish in the
neighbouring waters were they build always going a great distance
for their food – there is a good many builds their nests every year on
the Firdale trees in the Old Island pond at Milton   [A46, 175]

The Heronshaws build in the fir trees on the Island pond in Milton
gardens   they make their nests in clusters and associate like the rook
but their nests are of a more clumbsy and heavy appearance and yet
are perched on the tops of the trees and grains in such places that
appear incapable of bearing such a load of rough thorny sticks as
their nest appear below   Their eggs are long and very slender at the
small end of a greenish white colour spotted with brown and faintly
streaked with a paler colour – they never meddle with the fish in the
pond but go a great distance for their food   [A49, 74]

High overhead that silent throne
Of wild and cloud betravelled sky
That makes ones loneliness more lone
Sends forth a crank or reedy cry
I look the crane is sailing oer
That pathless world without a mate
The heath looked brown and dull before
But now tis more then desolate

[A57, 98]

*   *   *

The passer bye oft stops his horse to look
To see strange birds sit building like the rook
And every stranger ere he passes bye
Will stop and hollow shoo to see them flye
They swee about the trees a flopping herd
He goes and thinks them some outlandish bird
They bring their sticks nor fear the noisey clown
And load the trees till nearly broken down
They little think the crane will leave the floods
And make their nests like crows among the woods

HERON

They lay their sticks so thick each awkard guest
That boys might stand and walk from nest to nest
Their eggs are long and green and spotted brown
And winds will come and often throw them down

[B9, 97]

BITTERN

the bittern called here the butter bump from the odd loud noise
resembling that word haunts Whittlesea Mere lays in the reed shaws
– about the size of the Heron flyes up right into the sky morning and
evening and hides all day . . .   [A46, 175]

THE BUTTER BUMP

This is a thing that makes a very odd noise morning and evening
among the flags and large reed shaws in the fens   some describe the
noise as somthing like the bellowing of bulls but I have often heard it
and cannot liken it to that sound at all   in fact it is difficult to
describe what it is like   its noise has procurd it the above name by
the common people   the first part of its noise is an indistinct
muttering sort of sound very like the word butter utterd in a hurried
manner and bump comes very qu[i]ck after and bumps a sound on
the ear as if eccho had mockd the bump of a gun just as the mutter
ceasd nay this is not like   I have often thought the putting ones
mouth to the bung hole of an empty large cask and uttering the word
'butter bump' sharply woud imitate the sound exactly   after its first
call that imitates the word 'butter bump' it repeats the sound bump
singly several times in a more determind and louder manner – thus
'butter bu′mp b′u′mp b′u′m′p butter bu′mp'   it strikes people at
first as somthing like the sound of a coopers mallet hitting on empty
casks   when I was a boy this was one of the fen wonders   I usd
often to go on a sunday with my mother to see my aunt at peakirk
when I often wanderd in the fen with the boys a bird nesting and
when I enquird what this strange noise was they describd it as
coming from a bird larger then an ox that coud kill all the cattle in the
fen if it choose and destroy the villager likwise but that it was very
harmless and all the harm it did was the drinking so much water as to
nearly empty the dykes in summer and spoil the rest so that the stock
coud scarcly drink what it left   this was not only a story among
childern but their parents believd the same thing   such is the power
of superstition over ignorant people who have no desire to go

beyond hearsay and enquire for themselves but the 'world gets wiser
every day'   tis not believd now nor heard as a wonder any longer –
they say that it is a small bird that makes the noise not much unlike
the quail tho a deal larger and longer on the legs   they say it puts its
beek in a reed when it makes the noise that gives it that jarring or
hollow sound which is heard   so far I have no knowledge of its
using the reed but I believe they are right in the bird   I have startend
such a bird myself out of reed shaws myself were I have heard this
noise and afterwards the noise has been silent which convinced me
that the one was the bird   I never saw it but on the wing and it
appeard to me larger the[n] a pheasant of a li[ke] and not unlike it
either in shape or color but it flew different – there is a great many of
these birds on whittlesea mere and their noise is easily heard in a
morning on the London road which is some miles distant   its noise
continues all summer and at the latter end of the year it is silent and
heard no more till summer   [A46, 118]

Curlew Tribe

CURLEW

very common here in winter coming down with the floods
    they haunt Marshes and boggy heaths in summer and makes
their nests like the Pewit on the bare ground among rushes &c laying
from 3 to 5 eggs of a dirty white color   [A46, 176]

WOODCOCK

I have seen odd ones here till the beginning of may and I often
thought that such never went away but bred here   [A46, 176]

> Up flies the bouncing woodcock from the brig
> Where a black quagmire quakes beneath the tread*
>   [A48, 9]

SNIPE

Snipes are often seen with us in summer and their nests have been
found but I cannot say further   I saw one yesterday (12th of May) it
sat so close that I likend to set my foot on it   I examined the place
and I fancied it was preparing a nest in the midst of a large tuft of fog
or dead grass common on the heaths   [A46, 176]

* From 'Emmonsails Heath in winter'.

To the Snipe

Lover of swamps
The quagmire over grown
With hassock tufts of sedge – where fear encamps
Around thy home alone

The trembling grass
Quakes from the human foot
Nor hears the weight of man to let him pass
Where thou alone and mute

Sittest at rest
In safety neath the clump
Of hugh flag forrest that thy hants invest
Or some old sallow stump

Thriving on seams
That tiney islands swell
Just hilling from the mud and rancid streams
Suiting they nature well

For here thy bill
Suited by wisdom good
Of rude unseemly length doth delve and drill
The gelid mass for food

And here may hap
When summer suns hath drest
The mores rude desolate spungy lap
May hide they mystic nest

Mystic indeed
For isles that ocean made
Are scarcely more secure for birds to breed
Than this flag hidden lake . . .

[A47, 104; *see below pp. 92–4*]

COMMON GODWIT [BLACK-TAILED GODWIT]

very common about the fen   lays on the ground in tussocks* of
grass and rushes   [A46, 176]

* Clare has 'tuffocs'.

GREEN SHANK

known in the Fens near the Sea   [A46, 176]

RED SHANK

very common in the Fen about Oxney   [A46, 176]

Sandpiper Tribe

KNOT

very common in our fens   they lay on the ground like most other fen
birds   [A46, 176]

RUFFS AND REEVES

they [come] in great droves in spring to our fens and are caught in
netts   the male is calld a Ruff and the female a Reeve   they build on
the ground and breed here   [A46, 176]

The fowlers do not kill these birds when they catch them but make
them fat with wheat which they eat very readily   [A46, 180]

COMMON SANDPIPER

has been seen here   [A46, 176]

DUNLIN

unknown to me   [A46, 176]

PURRE [DUNLIN]

I have seen flocks of them about our meadows   they appear very
[   ] to the landscape sometimes turning their bellys and their
backs uppermost which shades white and black alternatly which has
a fine effect over the flooded meadows   [A46, 176]

PEEWIT [LAPWING]

they are as common as crows here in spring   they lay on the ground
and make no nest but use a horse footing or any hollow they can
find   they lay four eggs of an olive green color splashed with large
black spots and the narrow points of the eggs are always laid
inwards   they have a way of decoying any thing from their young or
nest by swopping and almost tumbling over before them as if

LAPWING

wounded and going to fall uttering their harsh screaming note but when near the nest they are silent and flye off in another direction which is always a signal to the old egg hunters that the nest is at hand   shepherds with us train their dogs to hunt the nests and many people make it their employment in spring to find them often getting as much as 3d apiece for the eggs   the young run as soon as they are out of the shells – Peewits are easily tamed and are often kept in gardens were they are said to do much good by destroying the slugs and worms on which they feed   [A46, 177]

The pewet hollos chewsit as she flyes
And flops about the shepherd where he lies
But when her nest is found she stops her song
And cocks [her] coppled crown and runs along

[A61, 8]

*   *   *

Agen the homstead hedge with brambles green
So quiet and in shelter so serene
Pewets in the sunshine dance about at play
When out afield tis called a bitter day

[A57, 12]

Plover Tribe

GOLDEN PLOVER

known in the fens   [A46, 177]

1828   A golden Plovers nest was found on southorp heath or at least 4 young Plovers for they make no nest – and they were taken to a clergy man at Barnack who ascertened what they were
1831   a young golden Plover was caught in the Pale grounds next oxey wood this summer by J Moor who took it to Milton   [A49, 83]

DOTTEREL

very numerous and well known in the fens were it breeds on the ground   [A46, 177]

RING DOTTEREL [RINGED PLOVER]

have been seen here   [A46, 177]

Rail Tribe

LAND RAIL [CORNCRAKE]
lay on the ground
the youg ones run as soon as they break thro the shell   [A46, 177]

> How sweet and pleasant grows the way
> Through summer time again
> While Landrails call from day to day
> Amid the grass and grain

CORNCRAKE

> We hear it in the weeding time
> When knee deep waves the corn
> We hear it in the summers prime
> Through meadows night and morn
>
> And now I hear it in the grass
> That grows as sweet again
> And let a minutes notice pass
> And now tis in the grain

Tis like a fancy every where
A sort of living doubt
We know tis somthing but it neer
Will blab the secret out

If heard in close or meadow plots
It flies if we pursue
But follows if we notice not
The close and meadow through

Boys know the note of many a bird
In their bird nesting bounds
But when the landrails noise is heard
They wonder at the sounds

They look in every tuft of grass
Thats in their rambles met
They peep in every bough they pass
And none the wiser get

And still they hear the craiking sound
And still they wonder why
It surely cant be under ground
Nor is it in the sky

And yet tis heard in every vale
An undiscovered song
And makes a pleasant wonder tale
For all the summer long

The shepherd whistles through his hands
And starts with many a whoop
His busy dog accross the lands
In hopes to fright it up

Tis still a minutes length or more
Till dogs are off and gone
Then sings and louder then before
But keeps the secret on

Yet accident will often meet
The nest within its way
And weeders when they weed the wheat
Discover where they lay

And mowers on the meadow lea
Chance on their noisey guest
And wonder what the bird can be
That lays without a nest

In simple holes that birds will rake
When dusting on the ground
They drop their eggs of curious make
Deep blotched and nearly round

A mystery still to men and boys
Who know not where they lay
And guess it but a summer noise
Among the meadow hay

                              [A57, 71]

The Landrail

Ive listened when to school Ive gone
That craiking noise to hear
And crept and listened on and on
But neer once gotten near
Ive trampled thro the unmown grass
And dreaded to be caught
And stood and wondered what it was
And very often thought

Some farey thing had lost its way
Nights other worlds to find
And hiding in the grass all day
Mourned to be left behind
I hardly dreamed it was a bird
Tho so I often guest
And when its summer call I heard
What rapture filled my breast

But Ive since found their eggs forsooth
And so we may agen
But great the joy I missed in youth
As not to find them then
For when a boy a new nest meets
Joy gushes in his breast
Nor would his heart so quickly beat
Were guineas in the nest

Ive hunted till the day has been
So vanished that I dare
Not go to school nor yet be seen
That I was playing there
So mid the wheat Ive made a seat
Upon an old mere stone
And hid and all my dinner eat
Till four o clock was gone

The clock was all I had to mind
Lest I should start too soon
And glad at heart Ive been to find
The sun slope down at noon
Craik craik the bird would often cry
Close to me were I sat
As if to teaze me

Imprisoned

[A53, 11]

WATER CRAIK [WATER-RAIL]
it is very scarce here but has be[en] seen and its nest found [A46, 177]

Gallinule Tribe

WATER HEN [MOORHEN]
they are very common with us   they make a nest of flags and bull
rushes lined with grass and place it on a branch of thorn or willow
that hangs over the stream and sometimes they make it on a clump of
bull rushes in the middle of the stream   they lay 9 eggs of a pale ash

color spotted with lilac and joccolate colored spots   the young ones
are coveverd with brown down and take the water as soon as they get
out of the shell   They build in old pits in the meadows and in lone
ponds about the closes if undisturbed . . .   [A46,178]

COOT

the coot is like the more hen in its habits but larger   it haunts lakes
in meadows and solitary marshes but never builds its nest in
branches that overhang the stream − it beats down a place in the
midst of a reed bed or flag clump and rests its nest on them that
touches the water   it lays a great number of eggs as many as 12 or 14
larger then the more hens of a dirty white color spotted with dull
spots   the nest is made of flags bullrushes and grass like the more
hens but it is wove together so stout as to resist the floods that
happen to rise while she sits on her eggs and if the nest looses its hold
of the rushes it floats on the top of the water like a boat and the old
one is said to sit on it unconserned but I have not seen this tho I have
found the nest landed on dry land as left by the floods with the eggs in
it unmolested − the young ones take to the water as soon as they leave
the shells and return to it at night like the more hen   These birds are
subject to lice which is so common to them that it has grown into a
saying that any thing filthy is 'as lousey as a coot'   [A46, 178]

SWIMMING BIRDS

Grebe or Diver Tribe

Great crested Grebe or ash colored loon called her[e] Gaunts –
common about the fen dykes and on Whittlesea Mere   [A46, 178]

EARD GREBE OR EARD DOBCHICK [BLACK-NECKED GREBE]

said to 'inhabit and breed in great numbers near Spalding'   [A46, 178]

BLACK AND WHITE DOBCHICK [SLAVONIAN GREBE]

found in the fens   [A46, 178]

LITTLE GREBE

one shot on Milton fishpond by Henderson   it dived and remained
under water for 10 minutes together   [A46, 178]

Tern Tribe or Sea Swallows

COMMON OR GREAT TERN

has been shot at Whittlesea Mere   [A46, 178]

HERRING GULL

said to be common about Boston   [A46, 178]

COMMON GULL OR SEA MEW

very common in the fens and marshes near the sea   [A46, 178]

WINTER GULL OR CODDY MODDY 'CAUDY MAUDY'
[COMMON GULL]

these Gulls come up in flocks to our meadows in flood time and feed
on somthing that it leaves   they dabble about as high as their knees
were it is shallow – there is an old ryhme about them but what it
aludes to I cannot say   [A46, 178]

BLACK HEADED GULL

said to build about Whittlesea Mere and Hobeach Marsh   [A46, 179]

SKUA OR BROWN GULL [IMMATURE HERRING/BLACK-BACKED GULL]

I think this bird answers to the description of one shot last winter by B Price   it had been seen feeding on carrion in the fields   [A46, 179]

Duck Tribe

HOOPERS [WHOOPER SWAN]

a bird with this name often flyes over our [   ] in droves like wild geese   [A46, 175]

WILD SWAN [WHOOPER/BEWICK'S SWAN]

they often go over here in large flocks flying in figures like wild geese but a great deal higher while one keeps uttering a horse noise

[A46, 179]

CANADA OR CRAVAT GOOSE

said to be common about boston   [A46, 179]

BARNACLE GOOSE [CANADA/BARNACLE GOOSE]

one shot by Henderson below Peterbro   [A46, 179]

GREY LAG OR COMMON WILD GOOSE

very common here were they are said to breed   Mr Pennant says he saw the buisness of Geese pulling baere and that they pulled goss-lings that were not above 6 weeks old   I have no hesitation in saying that Mr Pennant is a Liar*   [A46, 179]

SPANISH GOOSE

I think the wild ones are what we call Conks   [A46, 179]

. . . Conks as large as a tame goose with a longer neck and the body more slender flye in companys like wild geese and are of the same

* The custom of plucking geese is described by Thomas Pennant who claimed that goslings of just six weeks old had their tails plucked. The production of goose-feathers was a regular trade in Lincolnshire.

color a bluish grey but they have* this singular difference in their species a black preturberance on the top of their bills next to the head they are very common about the fens and often build their nests in the flags &c in Deeping fen when the gossaders hunt them and set the eggs under those of the tame goose and as the young brood grows up they disable their wings and keep them for breeders to cross with the tame ones selecting a conk gander for the tame geese or a tame gander for the conks and the breed thus crossd become very hardy to stand the weather and breed earlier they generally retain their color but the black protuberance on the bill wears aways and diminishes in the crossing to a speck which I believe they always retain and by which mark the gossaders know the breed

[A46, 126; *see also under* DUCKS, *below*]

WHITE FRONTED GOOSE

BEAN GOOSE

BRENT GOOSE

all these said to be common in the fens and marshes   [A46, 179]

DUCKS

Wild ducks have been known to build in our meadows – sea fowl are governd in their excurions by the wind   fowlers know by the wind when they will return to our cost and when they will leave it
a beautiful black bird of the duck or diver kind was shot in the river Nen this winter with a long pheasant like tail   my friend Artis says it is‡ very rare and calls it the scooter   it is caught now and then in the Netts of fishermen† and a species of this bird is eaten in lent by the catholics who reckon it more a kin to fish then flesh by the circumstance of it being taken in the netts oftener then by any other means . . .   [A46, 126]

The Snipe**

. . . Wigeon and teal
And wild duck – restless lot
That from mans dreaded sight will even steal
To the most dreary spot

* Clare has 'they if'.   † Clare has 'it it'.
‡ Clare has 'fisherman'.   * See p. 81.

92

Here tempest howl
Around each flaggy plot
Where they who dread mans sight the water fowl
Hide and are frighted not

Tis power divine
That heartens them to brave
The roughest tempest and at ease* recline
On marshes or the wave

Yet instinct knows
Not safetys bounds on trepid wing to shun
The firmer ground where skulking fowler goes
With searching dogs and gun

By tepid springs
Scarcely one stride across
Though brambles from its hedge a shelter flings
Thy safety is at loss

And never chuse
The little sinking foss
Streaking the moores where spa red water spews
From pudges fringed with moss

Free booters there
Intent to kill and slay
Startle with cracking guns the spreading air
And dogs thy hants betray

From dangers reach
Here thou art safe to roam
Far as these washy flag sown marshes stretch
A still and quiet home

Thy solitudes
The unbounded heaven extrems
And there my heart warms into higher moods
And dignifying dreams

* Clare has 'eash'.

In these thy haunts
Ive gleaned habitual love
From the vague world where pride and folly taunts
I muse and look above

And see the sky
Smile on the meanest spot
Giving to all that creep or walk or flye
A calm and cordial lot

Thine teaches me
Right feelings to employ
That in the dreariest places peace will be
A dweller and a joy

[A57, 104]

SCOTER [COMMON SCOTER]
one shot on the River Nen by Henderson   [A46, 179]

WILD DUCK [MALLARD]
common in the fens some have been known to breed in our meadows
make a curious nest – a half wild sort fly in crowds about the fens in
harvest and eat great quantitys of the mown corn – account of a
Decoy   [A46, 179]

[MALLARD]
Wild ducks always rise against the wind that is to face it they never
rise with it to have it behind them   [A49, 74]

As boys where playing in their schools dislike
And floating paper boats along the dyke
They laid their baskets down a nest to see
And found a small hole in a hollow tree
When one looked in and wonder filled his breast
And halloed out a wild duck on her nest
They doubted and the boldest went before
And the duck bolted when they waded oer
And suthied up and flew against the wind
And left the boys and wondering thoughts behind

94

MALLARD

The eggs lay hid in down and lightly prest
They counted more then thirty in the nest
They filled their hats with eggs and waded oer
And left the nest as quiet as before

[B9, 50]

SHOVELER

on[e] shot by Artis in the river Nen   [A46, 179]

WIDGEON

very common in the fens here   [A46, 181]

COMMON TEAL

common here in Winter   [A46, 181]

Pelican Tribe

CORMORANT

one shot here by Porter a schoolmaster on the high elm trees that
stood by long close pond in a hard frost   [A46, 181]

SOLON GOOSE [GANNET]

The winter before last one of Phillips draymen of the Common brew
house Stamford when coming to Helpston saw a strange large bird in
Pilsgate meadow by the brook and on going to it its wings were so
long that it was unable to rise before he got to it   it was about the
size of a Swan with a straight long bill about a foot long and a neck
longer then that of the swan   its eyes were of a bright blue its bill
and legs also were blue   it was web footed   the bird was of a dirty
white color all over excepting the wing feathers which were tipt with
black and a spot on the head of the same color   its wings were of an
immense awkard length compard with the size of the bird – it was
very fierce and attacted anything that approached it with undaunted
courage   the men said that it peckd very sharp and hurt them thro
their cloaths – a school master was at the public-house and tho he
had Pennants History he declared that he was unable to call it by its
name   I know not what became of the bird   the fellow talked of
making a present of it to his master   [A46, 127]

MYSTERY BIRDS

There has been a many strange bird seen about us for we live in a slip
between two shores and they are often tempted to cross from one
to the other   they generally come from the eastward towards the
west and one that has not found a place in books yet was shot three
or four Winters ago by a labourer   it was about the size of a large
goose but more slender in the body   it flew low and heavy like the
Puddock   its wings was very long and its neck about the length of a
goose   its eye was large and black and its bill black and hookd
exactly like an Hawk the upper mandable hooked over the other as if
for tearing its food   its legs were red striped with black and its feet
webed with odd large claws   its general color was white with light
wavings of brown all over like the breast of the Heron   [A46, 127]

[? *Pratincole*]

Saw four odd looking Birds like large swallows of a slate color on
their wings and back and their bellys white   they had forked tails
and long wings and flew exactly in the manner of the swallow but
instead of skimming along the ground they rose to a great height   I
frit them up from Swordy well a pond so called by the roman bank
which is never dry and often haunted by water birds   [A46, 127]

[Furze Lark, see p. 37]

97

GLOSSARY

agen, *prep.*, against
airiff, *n.*, cleavers or goose-grass;
   see also hairiff
awe, *n.*, haw
awthorn, *n.*, hawthorn

bard, *a.*, barred
bent, *n.*, coarse or wirey grass
bings, *n.*, bins
brig, *n.*, bridge
brinks, *n.*, banks of a stream
brun, *a.*, freckled or
   brown-coloured
brunny, *a.*, freckled or
   brown-coloured

carless, *a.*, careless
caudy maudy,
   coddy moddy, *n.*, herring gull
chanched, *v.*, chanced
chelped, *v.*, chirped
childern, *n.*, children
chinnying, *part.*, twittering,
   chattering
chittering, *part.*, chattering
churring, *part.*, whirring as of a
   nightjar
clauming, *part.*, clutching, seizing
clomb, *v.*, climbed
close, *n.*, small enclosed field
clumb, *v.*, climbed
coat piegon, *n.*, cote pigeon
copple, *n.*, crest of a bird
craiking, *part.*, creaking, croaking
crank, *a.*, sad, doleful, harsh
cranking, *part.*, sounding

crawking, *part.*, croaking
cronking, *part.*, croaking

daring-doing, *a.*, derring-doing
develing, *n.*, swift
dotterel, *n.*, pollard tree

eldern, *n.*, elder, *sambucus niger*
everdent, *n.*, evidence

farey, *n.*, fairy
field keeper, *n.*, game keeper
firdale, *n.*, fir tree
flirsts, *v.*, flirts
flower, *n.*, flour
fluskering, *part.*, flying with
   abrupt motion
flye, *n.*, flight
fog, *n.*, coarse grass
freckd, *a.*, freckled
frit, *a.*, frightened
frittered, *a.*, spotted, freckled

genrearly, *adv.*, generally
gossader, *n.*, gooseherd
gough, *n.*, gouging tool
grain, *n.*, branch of a tree
guest, *v.*, guessed
gurring, *part.*, onomatopoeic word
   for a chattering noise

hairiff, *n.*, cleavers, goose grass;
   see also airiff
hant, *n.*, haunt
hants, *v.*, haunts
heart, *v.*, heard
hilling, *part.*, covering, emerging

hollow, *v.*, hollo

horse, *a.*, hoarse

hugh, *a.*, huge

jelted, *v.*, thrown underhand with a sudden movement

joccolate, *a.*, chocolate

kecks, *n.*, dried stalks of umbellifers eg. cow parsley and hog weed. Often used of plant itself.

knarled, *a.*, gnarled

knaw, *v.*, gnaw

lair, *n.*, layer

lair, *v.*, hide

lap over, *v.*, overlap

led, *a.*, lead

leveret, *n.*, hare

like, *n.*, lark

lither, *a.*, lazy

loosing, *part.*, losing

lordship, *n.*, manor or parish

mozzled, *a.*, mottled

mow, *n.*, stack of corn or hay

nail passer, *n.*, corruption of 'nail-piercer', auger

newling, *n.*, new one

nimble, *v.*, to move quickly, nimbly

oddling, *a.*, odd

oddling, *n.*, odd one

pail, *n.*, paling

pined, *p.p.*, starved, famished

pink, *n.*, var. of spink, chaffinch

plashed, *p.p.*, splashed

pooty, *n.*, snail shell, particularly *Capaea nemoralis*

puddock, *n.*, kite

pudge, *n.*, puddle

raisin, *n.*, resin

ramping, *part.*, wild, luxuriant

recond, *v.*, reckoned

reedshaw, *n.*, sedge, reed-blade

rig, *n.*, ridge

rig tree, *n.*, roof ridge

sallow, *n.*, willow

scar, *v.*, scare

scard, *p.p.*, scared

scrat, *v.*, scratch

scotch, *n.*, stop

screeker, *n.*, screecher, rattle

sed, *p.p.*, said

sedge wobbler, *n.*, sedge warbler

shaw, *n.*, sedge or stalk

shoy, *a.*, shy

skreeking, *part.*, screeching, squeaking

sosh, *v.*, to dip suddenly in flight

sprote, *n.*, twig

starnel, *n.*, starling

stearing, *part.*, stirring

stoven, *n.*, stump

stragedee, *n.*, strategy

strunted, *p.p.*, stuck up in the air

stulp, *n.*, stump

stunt, *a.*, abrupt

stuntly, *adv.*, abruptly

suthied, *v.*, sighed

sutty, *a.*, sooty

swarmed, *a.*, covered

swees, *v.*, swings

swopping, *part.*, swooping

swopt, *v.*, swooped

tar marling, *n.*, mark made with tar

thuogh, *prep.*, though

tutling, *part.*, tootling

twitch, *n.*, coarse grass

twitchy, *n.*, like coarse grass

wews, *v.*, sighs

whewed, *v.*, sighed

white, *n.*, wight

wimble, *n.*, gimblet

womoan, *n.*, woman

INDEX